A Pare[illegible]to Family Separation

My Mum and Dad are Separating
Book Series

Marina Tsioumanis

newynpublishing

Other Books in the Series

My Mum and Dad are Separating, Children's Book

My Mum and Dad are Separating, Activity Book

This SECOND EDITION of
***A Parents' Guide to Family Separation* part of**
***My Mum and Dad are Separating* book series published in 2021 by**

Newyn Publishing

publisher@newynpublishing.com

First published as part of *Mum and Dad are Separating* in Great Britain in 2009 by
Speechmark Publishing Ltd, UK
www.speechmark.net
Cover image: Dolgachov©123rf.com

Tsioumanis, Marina

A Parents' Guide to Family Separation: My Mum and Dad are Separating

ISBN 978-0-6485075-0-5

Contents

Award-Winning Book!

Awarded 'Highly Commended' at the prestigious British Medical Association (BMA) Book Awards, 2009.

Preface

Dear Reader,

I am glad that you have chosen to read this book. It is designed to provide information about grief and the changes that many families encounter when going through family separation.

You yourself may be the parent or grandparent, another relative or a friend of a child who is experiencing family separation. You may be a professional who works with separating families, or perhaps you have recently separated from your partner and are looking for ways to help your family through the associated grief. This book will provide valuable information about how separation affects children and families and what you can do to nurture yourself, your family and the children involved.

I hope you find this book easy to read and useful.

Marina Tsioumanis

Acknowledgements

Thank you to my wonderful partner Alec for his love and encouragement and to my family and friends for their support. Thankyou also to Jude Aquilla and Gary MacRae for their valuable assistance with publishing the second edition of this book. A further thankyou to friends Liz Lane, Sam Haidar, and Sandra and Brian Massey.

I am most appreciative to Valerie Redman for allowing her previous work on 'Grief' and the 'Grief Curve' to be incorporated and adapted into this book.

Thank you to my friend and colleague Zoi Lekkas, for her teachings on self-nurturing techniques. Her work inspired me to develop and write the sections 'Skills for Developing Independence' and 'Strategies for Self Reliance'.

I would like to acknowledge the important work of Jennifer McIntosh, for her extremely valuable training on 'Child Inclusive Practice in Primary Dispute Resolution' and 'Children in Focus' (visit ChildrenBeyondDispute.com).

I also wish to note, with special thanks, the many clients and separating families with whom I have worked in various clinical and training settings. These include my private practice, and at UnitingCare Wesley, Port Pirie and Centacare Catholic Family Services, in Adelaide.

Finally, I offer my warmest thanks and gratitude to Speechmark Publishing for publishing the first edition of this book.

Introduction

A Parents' Guide to Family Separation offers in-depth information about and a comprehensive look at what happens throughout the process of family separation.

The information provided is intended to be both supportive and useful. The book offers a broad range of practical tools and strategies to help children and adults through their feelings of grief and process of adjustment. These are designed to be of benefit especially to parents who are separating, who will find them easy to apply. The book is also an appropriate resource for relatives of separating families and for professionals who work with children and separating families.

In places, the book addresses these three groups generally and inclusively, as in its entirety it has been written to appeal to all three audiences. In other places, however, the book leaves its general stance and addresses the separating parent directly. This approach has been utilised so that the grieving parent feels both personally comforted by the supportive tone of the book and that their personal experience of grief has been validated and acknowledged. Although addressing the parent, the text in these places is still also intended for relatives and professionals.

The book has been structured in three chapters, each of which focuses on different areas of family separation. In this way, the content of the book is designed to provide a clear and practical reference, as demonstrated below.

- Chapter 1 addresses 'Grief.' It begins with information about the stages of grief and about the different ways in which children and adults experience each stage of grief. It provides a full range of tips and strategies that readers can utilise to support grieving children and adults through their personal experience of grief.
- Chapter 2 addresses 'Family adjustments'. It details common reactions of children and adults to separation and provides strategies for explaining separation to children. It explains the common factors that arise during family separation and suggests helpful methods that adults can apply in order to minimise the impact of further stress on children. It explains ways to assist children to cope more effectively with the changes occurring in their family, and gives tips on promoting healthy development in children in the long term.
- Chapter 3 addresses 'Reframing family'. It provides information on building healthy

dynamics for the ongoing relationship of the family. It looks at how adults can parent together following separation and introduces helpful methods and ideas for assisting children to adjust to new contact arrangements with each parent. It addresses the potential impact that common factors of separation can have on children and refers to post-separation services available to children and separating families. The chapter contains many practical techniques that can promote family resilience and a healthy view of family post-separation.

The book is a valuable and rich resource for separating parents, their relatives and the professionals who work with children and separating families. It is comprehensive and full of information and practical tips for support. At the same time, it is simple to read and easy to understand and refer back to. It has been written in a supportive and caring tone, which is designed to promote a better sense of coping and well-being for the reader and for those for whose benefit the reader intends to use the information given.

Chapter 1

Grief

What does grief look like?

We often think about grief in terms of the specific loss associated with the death of a loved one. But people can experience grief reactions to a range of losses, including, for example: family breakdown; the break-up of a relationship; moving house; changing jobs; retirement; loss of income or status; or children leaving home. The information in this book is designed to inform and support families through the grief associated with family separation.

It is common knowledge among grief counsellors that no two people will ever grieve in exactly the same way. Nor will they experience the same situation in the same way. Human beings are subjective: they interpret their world and their experiences within it differently. Therefore, it follows that not only will people be affected differently by separation, but they will also react differently to it.

To be a support to a grieving child (or adult), it is not necessary that you understand how that person is grieving or coping. Instead, it is enough to be informed about grief, so that you can support and validate them in their unique experience of it.

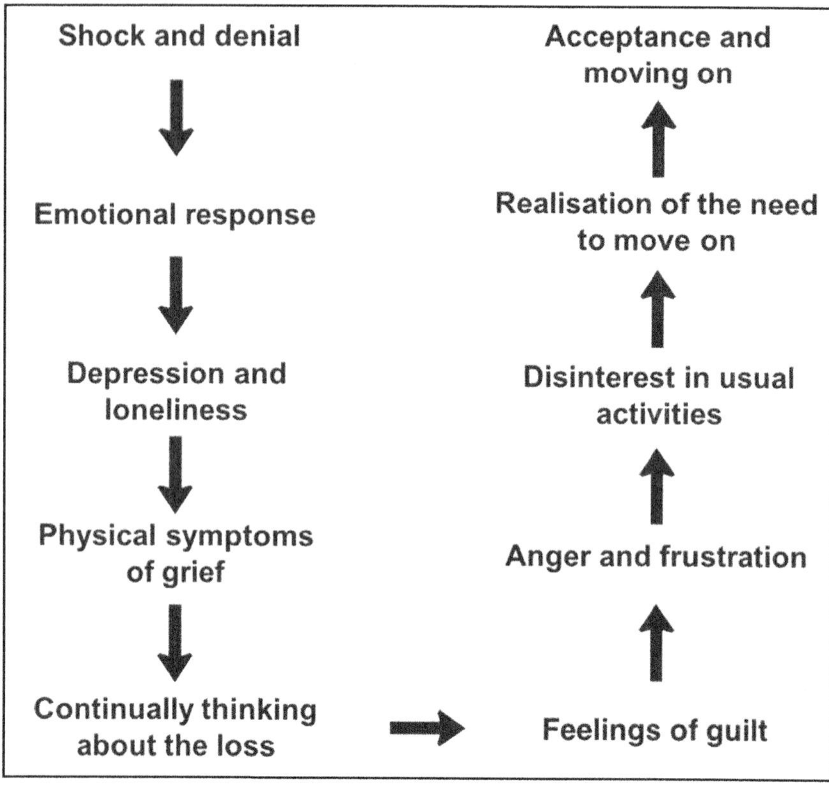

The grief cycle

Source: adapted from Valerie Redman, 2003, 'The Grief Curve' in Certificate IV *'Counselling Skills with Transactional Analysis'.* Original copyright © Redman Enterprises Pty Ltd, Glenelg South, South Australia. By permission.

To assist you in knowing about grief, you might like to have a look at one model of the cycle of grief shown in the diagram on the following page. You may or may not have seen a depiction of a grief cycle before, or even know what grief can look like for different people. There are many versions of the grief cycle. Some are available in books, others on the internet, and they may be available as handouts at community centres. They are an excellent resource for families. They provide valuable information about grief, and outline the common stages experienced in the grief process. Being informed about grief helps people accept their experience of grief. For example, grieving people commonly feel 'out of control' or 'overwhelmed' and wonder if they are 'going crazy'. Having knowledge of grief can provide reassurance; it helps to normalise it.

Grief cycles depict common stages of grief. They also provide flexibility. They allow for each person to grieve in their own way and at their own pace. The individuality and uniqueness of each person's experience of grief is valued and respected.

In a nutshell... What does grief look like?

- *People can experience grief reactions to a range of losses, including family separation.*
- *Grief cycles outline common stages experienced in the grief process.*
- *People who are grieving commonly feel 'out of control' and 'overwhelmed'.*
- *Being informed about grief helps people accept their experience of grief.*
- *Each person will grieve in their own way and at their own pace.*

The grief cycle

The cycle of grief depicted in the diagram is a representation of the grief commonly experienced by *adults*. Older children and adolescents will identify with many of the stages. Younger children will identify with some of them. Children grieve in different ways from adults. They experience grief 'stages', but in the context of their age and developmental skills. Further discussion of children's grief can be found later in this chapter and particularly in Chapter 2.

The diagram of the grief cycle shows that grief is not a static phase: it is neither constant nor motionless. Rather, as suggested above, there are many 'stages' to grief, and many different feelings, experiences and changes within these. People's experience of grief (how they think, feel, behave) may alter frequently: it may differ from day to day or moment to moment. Or it may remain the same for long periods of time.

The model presented comprises 10 stages of grief. Generally, people don't finish one stage and move on to the next in sequential order. Instead, they often tend to move back and forth between the stages. Sometimes they will find themselves experiencing several stages simultaneously. For instance, someone who has recently gone through family separation might find themselves experiencing each of the second, fourth and fifth stages at the same time.

Adults generally take anywhere between six months and two or three years to progress through the grief cycle. Children's grief varies in duration, depending on many factors, including their age, their access to support, their ongoing relationship with their parents, and other changes that family separation might have made to their life.

The next section looks in detail at the 10 stages of grief depicted in the diagram of the grief cycle. It begins with the first stage, that of shock and denial

In a nutshell... The grief cycle

- *Children grieve in different ways from adults; they experience grief 'stages', but in the context of their age and developmental skills.*
- *Grief is not a static phase: people's experience of it alters frequently.*
- *People tend to move back and forth between grief stages; sometimes they will experience several stages at the same time.*
- *Adults generally take from six months to two or three years to progress through the grief cycle; children's grief varies in duration depending on many factors, including their age.*

The 10 stages of grief

Grief stage 1: shock and denial

This is often experienced as numbness. It can last for minutes or days or longer. It can come and go. Some people feel literally 'frozen' and find it hard to speak, move or think, or to focus clearly on anything. They have a sense of being detached from themselves, from their situation and from others around them. Sometimes, people in this stage will feel themselves becoming frantic, or compelled to 'do something'. They might feel the need to clean, pace around the house, talk excessively, be with other people, or cling to routines. Staying busy helps to keep thoughts and emotions at bay.

Children will usually engage in fantasy, wishing or make-believe to maintain their denial of the separation. They often cling to the fantasy that their parents will reunite, and they make up stories to explain the absence of the parent who has left.

Generally, this stage is one of emotional overload. People feel overwhelmed by the enormity of what is happening. They respond to the stress by temporarily blocking out the reality of the situation. They deny the situation, or aspects of it. They do this to protect themselves from feeling the full impact of the pain of their loss. They are unsure how to cope with or process what is occurring, and feel that they cannot accept it. They might respond by refusing to believe it, by resisting it, or by going 'blank'. All these reactions are a normal part of the grieving process.

When people come out of shock and denial they usually go straight into stage 2: emotional response.

In a nutshell... Shock and denial

- *People might feel numb for a while, finding it hard to speak, move, think or act.*
- *Alternatively, they might react by becoming frantic, feeling the need to clean, pace, talk excessively, or cling to people or routines.*
- *Children usually engage in fantasy, wishing or make-believe to maintain their denial or explain their parent's absence.*
- *Generally, people feel overwhelmed and unable to accept what is happening.*

Grief stage 2: emotional response

The hallmark of the emotional response stage is that a person starts crying and is unable to stop. The floodgates open. The emotions that they tried to 'block' while in the shock and denial phase come to the surface and are experienced. This is often a time of sadness, pain, turmoil, loneliness, ache and emotional suffering. It too is a normal and healthy part of grieving. It will be as long or short lived as it needs to be: there is no right or wrong duration. It will also be revisited as many times as necessary for healing in this stage. Often, people think they are 'over the crying' only to find that minutes, weeks, months or even years later, they return to it - again and again and again as the need arises.

Allowing yourself to cry is very healthy. It enables your body to release pent-up energy and emotion. At the same time, it might feel quite frightening. Tears might be uncontrollable, and the feeling of losing control might be alarming. You might instead choose to mask your feelings, or deny that you have any. You might cover your feelings of sadness with those of shame ('It's not okay to cry') or fear ('If I start crying I might go to pieces').

Unfortunately, the temptation for some people to 'put on a brave face' and 'hold themselves together' overrides any expression of grief. This is a common response in those who try to deny their grief to themselves. The tears and emotion become buried under layers of bottled-up grief. Bottling up grief is not healthy either for the body or for the mind. When people attempt to suppress their grief, it doesn't vanish. Instead, it often presents in unhealthy or destructive ways at a later time.

Another common response on the part of both parents and children is to put on a brave face in order not to upset other members of the family. So often, parents hide their grief from their children. They want to *be strong for their children's sake* and hold the family together. Amazingly, children, too, often suppress their emotions. They don't want to upset, or further upset, their parents or siblings.

It is all right for children to see parents cry. But, parents need to be mindful of how much and to what degree they display their distress to their children. They need to observe the impact their sadness has on them. It is not a good idea, for instance, for parents to cry for hours in front of their children. Doing so will create stress, confusion and anxiety in them. If you are in this situation, tell your children that you feel sad, let them know you cry, and show them that expressions of grief are acceptable. Tell them that it is all right for them to cry too, and to turn to you with their grief: that you will understand and support them.

Children will mirror what parents teach them. Masking your emotions and 'acting strong' will send a powerful message to them, about how to experience their own grief. Allowing grief to be talked about and experienced, on the other hand, informs children that their feelings are recognised and normal. It tells them that they can grieve and be supported.

Emotional release is a normal and healthy part of the grieving process. Sadness can be accepted, normalised and expressed in healthy ways.

In a nutshell... Emotional response

- *It is normal and healthy to experience a range of emotions.*
- *Suppressed grief will often present itself in unhealthy or destructive ways later.*
- *Crying excessively in front of children will create stress, confusion and anxiety in them.*
- *Tell children that it is all right for them to cry and that you cry and feel sad too.*
- *Children mirror what they are taught: 'acting strong' teaches them to mask their own emotions.*

Grief stage 3: depression and loneliness

In this stage of the grief cycle, people feel totally alone. They think that nobody can possibly understand or feel what they are going through. They may be surrounded by a house full of people and yet still feel alone. Lack of motivation, wanting to spend all day in bed, and feeling sick and unwell are normal, typical reactions. This phase might be likened to the turtle that withdraws its head into its shell to cocoon itself. It is usually an unpleasant time for everybody who experiences it, but it is also an important one.

Withdrawing, and retreating into yourself, allows you space and privacy in which to *feel* your grief and begin to process it. Children too become withdrawn and may feel isolated at stages of their grief. Sometimes, however, children are not withdrawing simply to experience grief feelings in a *healthy* way. Rather, they are engaging in *un*healthy withdrawal and avoidance. For example, developmentally, school-aged children don't like to be perceived to be different from their friends. At a time of grief, you might observe them repressing their feelings of grief and acting as though they are 'fine'. Verbally, they might also say that they are 'fine'. Withdrawal in this instance is being used as a way of containing and masking their feelings. It often leads to greater isolation, as children struggle to cope with their emotions on their own.

If you are in this stage of the grief cycle you may like to incorporate some structure and support into your day, to avoid becoming 'bogged down' in the isolation of it. Do this by encouraging yourself to establish small routines, such as sitting in the garden for a few minutes, walking around the block after breakfast, making a daily phone call to a friend. Activities like these help to create a framework for the day and allow you to receive some support at a difficult time.

Building in some 'one-on-one' time with your children is a useful way in which you can help them, too, to gain support and structure. Recognise their need for space, and avoid asking too many questions about how they feel because this can be intimidating and may cause them to withdraw even further. It is better to ask some general questions, incorporating an activity into the discussion, so that children don't feel 'boxed in'.

In a nutshell... Depression and loneliness

- *Feeling isolated is common; people think no one else can understand their grief.*
- *Lack of motivation and wanting to spend all day in bed are normal reactions.*
- *Children also become withdrawn and may feel isolated.*
- *School-aged children don't like to be viewed as different from their peers; they may act as though they are 'fine', even when they are not.*
- *Incorporating some structure into the day helps to counteract the isolation of this stage.*

Grief stage 4: physical symptoms of grief

Grief can be exhausting. It uses up a lot of energy. People often feel tired and weak for a period of time. They might also have difficulty falling asleep, instead lying awake tossing and turning. Or they might sleep easily for a few hours, but then wake to toss and turn until morning. Lack of sleep further exhausts an already tired and drained body. Many people comment on feeling like a 'walking zombie' - tired and yet unable to rest. This experience is unpleasant, but it is normal for this stage of grief. Other symptoms include: loss of appetite; loss of motivation (things that were once of interest no longer appeal); difficulty concentrating and thinking clearly; tightness around the chest; headaches and migraines; back ache; sore muscles; tingling; butterflies in the stomach; and nausea. These too are all very normal, typical responses to grief.

Young children might display any of the following: changes in eating and/or sleeping habits; changes in mood (they might be more irritable, for example); stomach/digestive problems; shorter attention span; or clinging and dependency. Visiting the family doctor for a check-up might be advisable during this stage of grief.

If your children are grieving, you may wish to inform their school of this. Anticipate changes in school performance: you might need to negotiate a temporary reduction in some of their school work and other activities.

A grieving person (child or adult) might find it helpful to sleep for a while in the afternoon as this allows their body to get some rest, especially if they are getting little or no sleep at night. Someone who has lost their appetite, or is discouraged by cooking or heavy meals, may prefer light food, such as warm soup, prepared for them. This will give their body some energy and strength, and is a simple way by which they can care for themselves at a time when they don't have much energy to give to that.

Gentle massages and back rubs can alleviate some of the tensions stored in muscles and the back. It helps young children to settle and communicates love, care and affection. Keeping the environment relaxed and quiet may help those suffering from headaches and migraines.

Parents might find that some household routines are put on hold for a while. It isn't necessary to keep up with all the washing, cleaning, committee meetings, school work, sporting events, and so on. In time, these activities will be resumed naturally. In the interim, parents might rely on helpful support from family, friends and neighbours to keep the more vital routines going.

In a nutshell... Physical symptoms of grief

- *Physical reactions, such as lack of motivation and reduced appetite, are normal.*
- *Children might display changes in eating or sleeping habits; they might become more irritable or clingy and experience digestive problems.*
- *Inform your child's school that your child is grieving and expect some changes in school performance.*
- *Expect disruption to routines and that some household tasks will be put hold*

Grief stage 5: continually thinking about the loss

In this stage people continually think, over and over again, about what has happened. They constantly revisit what was said and how they felt. Thoughts beginning with 'What if...?' and 'If only ...' are common. Sometimes people feel overwhelmed by these thoughts; they find it hard to switch them off. The thoughts keep turning round and round in their heads.

Some people comment that these thoughts are more frequent at night when they are in bed, or when they are alone, without work, school or activities to distract them. This too is a very normal and typical response to grief and doesn't mean that someone is 'going crazy' (which, as mentioned earlier, is a common fear people have in this stage). The constant flow of thoughts occurs because the grieving person is processing (sorting, thinking through, analysing) what has happened. Processing is how people attempt to make sense of what has gone on. It is how they try to begin to come to terms with it.

Children are very good at compartmentalising their lives. This means that they can put different areas of their life into different 'boxes' and focus on only one area at a time. This enables them to put grief away for a while. They get out their colouring books, play outside or visit friends. They then return to grief later.

Parents might see their children playing and mistakenly believe that they are adjusting well to the separation, or are no longer grieving. It is important to know that even if children seem to be all right, they are still grieving. Avoid jumping to the conclusion that they are 'fine' because they are happy at school each day, or had fun at the weekend. Find ways to open the channels of communication with them and let them know that all such feelings are normal and acceptable.

Very young children don't have the cognitive (or thinking) skills to process this stage very well. It is likely that they will express their confusion through their behaviour. Common displays include acting out, biting, hitting, kicking, tantrums, clinging, sulking and bullying. Recognise children's confusion and reassure them that they are loved. Provide stability and affection, and maintain routines to help them feel safe. Similar behaviour is also displayed by older children. Often, when they don't feel safe or comfortable talking about their feelings, they externalise them through their behaviour instead.

Children have concrete thinking, known as 'black and white' thinking. Generally, they will not understand the 'grey' situations in life, so it is important to keep explanations simple. You might ask them to repeat what you have told them in order to check how much of your explanation they have understood. You can also expect young children, between the ages of three and six, to ask 'why' questions over and over again. They will need you to repeat your explanations to help them comprehend what is happening.

This stage of the cycle can last for days, weeks or months. It is not uncommon for it to last for weeks at a time and then to reduce or stop. It may be revisited at various times during the grieving process. Keeping a diary can be useful because it allows people to get their thoughts down on paper. Children may like to draw in a diary instead.

Counselling or talking to a friend can also be useful at this stage. It allows the grieving person to externalise their thoughts, with support to process them.

In a nutshell... Continually thinking about the loss

- *It is normal to think repeatedly about what has happened.*
- *Thoughts beginning 'What if...?' and 'If only' are typical in this stage.*
- *Children compartmentalise their lives and focus on one area at a time; they put their grief on hold for a while and return to it later.*
- *Young children don't have the cognitive skills to process this stage well; they are likely to express their confusion through their behaviour.*

Grief stage 6: feelings of guilt

This is an extension of the processing common to the previous stage. In this stage, however, people blame themselves. Self-talk can take the form of 'If only I'd ...' and 'What if I'd ...?' This occurs as a result of 'over-processing', and is normal. People need to go through this phase, and to get their feelings of guilt 'out of their system'.

If you are going through this stage, you may find it helpful to think of all the reasons why you might blame yourself, and perhaps write these down. People in this stage may feel wretched for a while, but they are usually able to come out of it when they see that they cannot keep feeling that way indefinitely. You may find it helpful to have some things to hand with which to nurture yourself, so that you can bring yourself back into balance and improve your sense of wellbeing. You might also use positive affirmations, such as 'You did your best' and 'You are only human'. These can help to reduce the extent to which you blame or berate yourself.

Children too will experience this stage. Developmentally, children under the age of five tend to be egocentric (believing that the world and everything in it revolves around them). This means not only that they will see that everything that is happening is happening *to* them, but also that they might believe that what occurs in their life has occurred *because of* them. This in turn can translate into their believing that they '*caused*' their parents' separation. Adults know this is not the case, of course, but unlike adults, children of this age are generally unable to see beyond themselves, and so they 'personalise' the situation.

Blaming others is another way in which children address their feelings of guilt. They project the guilt they feel on to their parents. They blame their parents. They usually direct their blame at the parent with whom they live most of the time, or at the parent with whom they feel most comfortable.

Reassure children that the separation was not caused by them. Provide plenty of love, care and stability. If a parent argues or disagrees with their ex-partner, this should be done when young children cannot witness it. When young children see their parents arguing, they don't process this as 'Mum and Dad are arguing'. Rather, they decide: 'Mum and Dad must be arguing because of me ... I did something to cause it.'

As children get older they come to realise that they are not the centre of the world and things don't happen because of them. They will grow out of that early phase. But for young children, this is how they usually see the world. So, comfort and reassure them. Provide an environment for them that is as secure and non-argumentative as possible.

In a nutshell... Feelings of guilt

- *It is normal to feel guilty and blame yourself for a while; self-talk usually takes the form of 'If only I'd ...' and 'What if I'd ...?'*
- *Affirm that you 'did your best' and 'are only human'.*
- *Children under five are egocentric, believing that everything that happens in their life occurs because of them.*
- *Children can express guilt by blaming others and punishing one or both parents.*
- *Explain to children why the separation is occurring and tell them they are not to blame.*
- *Avoid arguing or disagreeing in front of your children; this increases their guilt and raises their anxiety.*

Grief stage 7: anger and frustration

Some people will find this a very difficult stage and will do their best to avoid it. Others will find themselves in it almost immediately. This is a time of anger, hostility and resentment. It is directed at other people (or an individual person), the situation and the person themselves. Some people will find it easy to feel anger towards themselves, but be reluctant to feel angry with the other people involved. Others will blame other people for their loss, but choose not to feel angry with themselves.

Understanding the distinction between healthy and unhealthy expressions of anger is not only useful but also important here. Anger itself is a normal emotion: it is normal for adults to feel angry with their ex-partner, friends and relatives, their children and themselves. Feeling anger is also a very important part of grief. As with crying, it allows the pent-up energy and emotion to be released. But what is the difference between unhealthy and healthy expressions of anger?

Unhealthy expressions of anger include, for example, threatening to hurt or harm or actually harming another person or yourself; screaming and yelling at another person; being destructive; and name calling. Although these responses might make you feel good at the time, they cause damage to relationships, to other people and to property.

Healthy expressions of anger occur when you acknowledge to yourself that you feel angry and allow yourself to be angry in a way that doesn't cause harm to yourself, others or property. You can still release pent-up feelings by punching a pillow or a punching bag, kicking a cardboard box, screaming loudly in your car, but these are not destructive in the way that unhealthy expressions of anger are. Talking about anger and validating it is also helpful.

Teaching children the difference between unhealthy and healthy anger is important. You can do this by asking them to hit the 'anger pillow' when they feel angry. Give them space and privacy to do so. You could also suggest that they draw a picture of their anger, or of a situation they feel angry about. You will find activities in the *My Mum and Dad are Separating, Activity Book* to which you can refer and that you can use with children.

Because anger is a normal emotion and a typical response to grief, it is important when grieving to allow yourself and others to feel angry. Telling people not to feel angry teaches them to bury their anger. It doesn't help them to release it in healthy ways. Suppressed anger always finds a way of coming out and usually does so in an unhealthy expression - in violence, for instance. Healing can occur only when the emotions that arise in grief can be expressed and dealt with. Burying them doesn't assist healing. Instead, it creates a 'pressure cooker' of repressed energy, which threatens to build and, eventually, to explode.

It is normal for children to feel angry with one parent, both parents, relatives, themselves or the situation, at one time or another. Some children will not express their anger directly at their parents. Instead, they will take it out on siblings or children at school, or passively, by withdrawing. If a child does express anger towards their parents, this will usually be directed, as with feelings of guilt, at the parent the child feels most comfortable with and least threatened by, or the parent the child usually lives with.

Tantrums are a common method young children use to attract an adult's attention and get their needs met. Sometimes toddlers feel frightened by their anger. They are too young to understand it or know how to manage it on their own. They need you to help them manage it. When they are calm, ask them what they were trying to tell you when they were angry. Teach them how to ask verbally for what they need.

Following the release of anger, or following anger exercises, a grieving person will usually start to feel sad and seek to be held and comforted. Be prepared for tears because there could be a revisit to stage 2 of the grief cycle. If you yourself are grieving, you might want to ask to be comforted during this time. A sense of tiredness will usually follow, and the grieving person might want to sleep. They have just used an enormous amount of energy, releasing their anger and sadness. They need a quiet space in which to rest and restore their energy.

Explore your own attitude to anger. Were you brought up in a household where *unhealthy* expressions of anger, such as violence, were expressed? If so, does witnessing your children's *healthy* anger retraumatise you? Do you re-experience the fear you felt in your own childhood? If you do, you might find that counselling support would be beneficial. Counselling can help people heal past experiences of unhealthy anger and, in turn, assist their children to express their healthy anger.

In a nutshell... Anger and frustration

- *It is normal to feel anger, hostility and resentment.*
- *Teach children the difference between unhealthy and healthy expressions of anger.*
- *Children usually direct their anger at the parent they live with or feel most comfortable with, or at siblings or children at school; they may respond passively, by withdrawing.*
- *Toddlers feel frightened by their anger; they need help to understand and manage it.*
- *When children calm down, ask them what they were trying to tell you when they were angry.*
- *Anger usually covers sadness, so be prepared for tears following the release of anger.*

Grief stage 8: disinterest in usual activities

When people grieve, they often feel that their life has been put on hold: that it revolves around their grief and the details of their separation. Often, just getting through the day can be a strain because the grieving process requires so much energy. Not surprisingly, then, it can be very difficult for individuals and families to return to their usual activities. Their life is no longer the way that it was before the separation. For some families the change is an improvement, for others this isn't the case. But whether or not the change is for the better, rebuilding and re-establishing a family following separation can be a long and gradual process. There is no 'quick fix' solution.

As noted earlier, most people comment that it takes anywhere from six months to two or three years to progress through grief. It is therefore normal for the process of rebuilding a family and returning to usual activities to take time. There are some activities, of course, over which you may have little control. For example, you might have to continue to work, whether or not you feel up to it, and your children will have to attend school. However, other activities will be within your control, and rather than trying to push yourself, move at your own pace. Grief is a slow process.

Some children may display disinterest in usual activities that is not attributable to lack of interest or motivation. They might be attempting to avoid grief. Think, for example, about a girl, perhaps, who used to attend swimming lessons with her father, but her father is no longer able to take her. Developmentally, she is of an age when children want to be like their friends. She worries about being seen to be different, and doesn't want to explain that her parents have separated. She feigns disinterest in swimming and avoids both it and other activities that might provoke similar situations. Whether you are her parent, a relative or a professional, invite her to look for solutions, either with you or with her other parent. Being seen as one of the crowd is very important to school-aged children, and needs to be kept in mind when you are talking to them.

In a nutshell... Disinterest in usual activities

- *When people grieve, they often feel that their life has been put on hold; that it revolves around the grief and details of the separation.*
- *Rebuilding a family following separation can be a long and gradual process.*
- *Don't push yourself: grief is a slow process.*
- *If children display disinterest in usual activities, which is not attributable to lack of interest or motivation, they might be attempting to avoid grief so they are not viewed as different from their peers.*

Grief stage 9: realisation of the need to move on

Gradually, people come to see that they cannot maintain their state of grief indefinitely. They have an awareness of what their life will look like when they emerge from their grief and endeavour to rebuild their lives without their partner. They may not be ready to do it yet, but there are glimpses of the light at the end of the tunnel. They feel more able to cope and to adjust to their new way of life.

People who are concerned that they are getting 'bogged down' in grief, or who would like support in moving forward, can find support through post-separation counselling, which is usually available for both adults and children. Some services may also offer counselling support over the telephone. The governing body operating in your country or nation might be able to supply information and advise on referral pathways for services providing post-separation counselling and other relevant support.

In a nutshell... Realisation of the need to move on

- *People come to realise that they cannot maintain their state of grief indefinitely.*
- *They feel more able to adjust to their new way of life.*
- *Those who would like support in moving forward can find this through post-separation counselling.*

Grief stage 10: acceptance and moving on

How do you know when you have 'moved on'? Each person will decide that for themselves, and each person's definition and expectations of 'moving on' will be different. It is unlikely that there will be a distinct, defining moment. Instead, progression will be gradual and the time it will take will vary.

There are likely to be some distinguishing signs along the way. Common markers that most people can relate to include: things gradually falling into place; an increased sense of coping; a lessening of raw emotions; an emerging sense of well-being and completeness; an increased sense of 'I' rather than 'we'; a letting go; an acceptance; a new way of relating; and a redefinition of family.

We can think about this by comparing two imaginary canvases. One canvas is a detailed picture. You see it, know it, it's tangible. This is the picture of your family before separation. You know what it looked like at the time and how it felt to be part of that picture. It was predictable. You want to cling to it. The other canvas is blank. It represents your family post-separation. It is unfamiliar. You want to resist it.

Grief places you at a position between the two canvases. You can't go back and you can't move forward. For a while, you don't belong in either picture. You are suspended in an in-between place. In this place, you begin to disconnect gradually from the old picture of life. You cry, make some decisions, feel stuck, question what happened, retreat into yourself. Occasionally, you glance over at the blank canvas - the one that is to be your life of the future. You don't know what that picture will look like. You don't know if you will cope and whether you will be all right.

Eventually, things start to fall into place. Small decisions made daily emerge as splashes of colour on the blank canvas. Gradually, the post-separation picture starts to fill out. During the slow grieving period, the picture gains definition. People, things and routines emerge on the print. You begin to see a picture of what life post-separation will look like. You step on to the canvas, and gradually accept that this is to be your life: new, and different from the previous one.

Moving on is about living in the new picture. The new picture becomes your new reality and new reference point. Your initial desire to cling to the familiar picture of old subsides. Its contents have been sifted and sorted: into those that are left behind and those that are dusted off and carried into the new. Memories of the past can now be celebrated from the platform of life that is the new canvas, with its splashes of colour and promise of hope.

In a nutshell... Acceptance and moving on

- *Each person's expectations of 'moving on' will be different.*
- *Moving on will usually be experienced as a gradual process.*
- *Grief locates people in a place between two canvases.*
- *One canvas is full of detail and represents the life they knew; they often cling to this.*
- *The other is hazy and unknown, and represents the future; at first people avoid it, then start to make decisions, develop routines and fill it in - they are moving on.*

Grief and other aspects of daily life

A second diagram of grief entitled 'Grief and other aspects of daily life interwoven' has been provided. Here, the stages of grief are the same, but, in contrast to the grief cycle, are randomly contained within a semi-permeable circle of grief. A grieving person can experience the 'stages' of grief at any time, and all

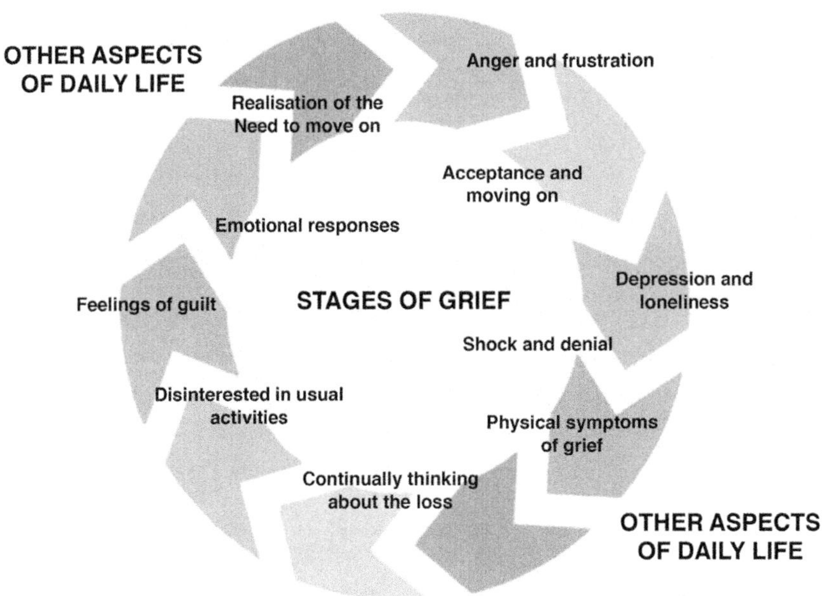

Grief and other aspects of life interwoven

Source: adapted from Valerie Redman, 2003, 'The Grief Curve' in Certificate IV *'Counselling Skills with Transactional Analysis'*. Original copyright © Redman Enterprises Pty Ltd, Glenelg South, South Australia. By permission.

stages are equally important; as was emphasised earlier, to experience them is a normal part of the grieving process. The semi-permeable circumference of the circle also demonstrates that grief is an experience people move in and out of. It shows that the 'stages' of grief are contained within the experience of grief, but that grief is interwoven with all other aspects of a person's life.

Two diagrams of grief have been included in this book to indicate that there is not just one way to grieve. There are many ways to experience the grief process and you are encouraged to find the diagram of grief that best fits you and your experience of your grief.

In a nutshell... Grief and other aspects of daily life

- *Grief is interwoven with all other aspects of a person's life.*
- *There is more than one way to grieve, as illustrated by the two diagrams of grief in this chapter.*
- *People are encouraged to find a diagram of grief that best fits their experience of grief.*

Layers of grief

Separation usually produces a layering of grief; that is, a multitude of changes, layered one on top of another. First, there is grief over family breakdown. Sometimes grief will be associated with seeing less of relatives, or with moving house. There may be a move out of the neighbourhood, or a loss of friendships, or changes to income. Children, for example, may grieve over seeing less of one or both parents, over parents working longer hours, or over changing school and losing friends.

It is important to be aware that children will be grieving over some or all of the changes that separation has brought about, and that for each change, not only will they be at different points on the grief cycle, but they will move through grief at different rates. Therefore, by keeping as many things as possible the same as they were before the separation, children can be protected from experiencing further layers of grief. For example, seek to keep children in the environment they know, around the people they know, and following the same routines. If this is not possible, at least be aware that they will experience grief as a result of each change that is made, and offer appropriate support and time for adjustment.

However, this is not to say that changes cannot or should not be made. With support, children can adapt quite well to change, whereas in contrast, trying to hold on to situations that are not working can be more detrimental to children in the long run. Therefore, be willing to provide support to children at times of increased impact that any additional change might have on them.

In a nutshell... Layers of grief

- *Separation usually produces a layering of grief.*
- *Attempt to keep as many things as possible the same for children.*
- *Be aware that grief will be encountered for each change that is made; appropriate support and time for adjustment should be offered.*

Goodbye ceremonies

Death involves many rituals and ceremonies designed to mark an opportunity to say goodbye - funerals, wakes and memorial services all act as goodbye ceremonies. Saying goodbye is very important both to the grief process and to healing.

Separation does not have any 'social' rituals or ceremonies associated with it, to help families say goodbye to their 'family' as they knew it. You might therefore like to consider some ceremonies you could incorporate into your grieving process. This might involve 'saying goodbye' to each room in the house before you move out or put it up for sale. It might involve planting a tree as a symbol for the 'new family' you will become, creating a 'memory box' of favourite family moments, or writing a poem of goodbye. Children might have their own suggestions for how they would like to say goodbye.

Unlike death, which is final, separation is a stage between two ways of 'being a family'. You are still a family, but in a different way. The dynamics of the family have changed and it is the old dynamics that you are saying goodbye to. In time, a new definition of family will emerge, with new dynamics, and family members will find a new way of relating to one another.

In a nutshell... Goodbye ceremonies

- *Separation doesn't have any associated 'social' ceremonies to help families say 'goodbye' to their family as they knew it.*
- *Consider some ceremonies you could incorporate into the grieving process.*
- *Unlike death, which is final, separation is a stage between two ways of 'being a family'; in time new family dynamics will emerge.*

Chapter 2

Family Adjustments

Eleven common parenting perils

Childhood is such a brief interval in the human lifespan. We like to think of it as a time free from worries, pressures and deadlines. In reality, though, many children face upheavals and difficult life events in the course of their childhood. How well they get through them often depends on the support they receive from their families. Separation rates high on the list of stressful life events, not far below the death of a family member. Children need to be supported through separation, and every attempt should be made to avoid either directly or indirectly shouldering them with 'adult' worries or responsibilities.

Separation requires adults and children to make many decisions about how to cope, what to do and how to do it. A lot of energy is used in devising strategies for coping and in making the separation more *manageable* and *bearable*. Parents do their best to make healthy, positive decisions. Invariably, however, as a result of the strain they are under and perhaps their reduced resources, they also make some decisions that put added stress on to their children. Similiarly, because children have limited resources and minimal life skills, many of the decisions they make to cope with the situation are detrimental to themselves.

This section outlines common *maladaptive* coping strategies, utilised for varying lengths of time by parents and children. Many parents, in their grief, may be unaware of the added stress these scenarios can put on to their children. What follows has been included in order to encourage reflection and thought on the impact the scenarios described might have on children, and to help parents to make the best possible decisions for their family at a very stressful time. It is not intended to be in any way judgemental.

In a nutshell... Parenting perils

- *Separation rates high on the list of stressful life events; parents do their best through this difficult time, so look for ways to support your children through it.*
- *Separation requires adults and children to make many decisions about how to cope.*
- *Sometimes maladaptive coping strategies emerge, which invariably place added stress on children, of which parents are often unaware*

Parenting peril 1: when children become the nurturing parents

Some children take on a parental and nurturing role, comforting and supporting their parents through grief (often hiding their own pain and 'acting strong' in an attempt not to upset their parents further). Children as young as three have taken on nurturing roles. Typically, this is displayed when parents express emotions such as sadness. The child masks their own sadness, reaching out to touch or hug the parent, and to reassure them that things will get better.

If this is occurring often, parents might try not to cry or grieve openly when their children are nearby to witness it. It can be detrimental to children to feel unable to grieve themselves because they are so busy acting as a support to their parents. Some children (typically boys aged 8-11 years) may say that they don't want to cry, because their mother or father is very distressed and crying will only make things worse for their parent. It is easy to see the potential problems that might develop if this behaviour continues - for example, masking grief doesn't allow healing to take place. Unresolved grief like this can impact on many areas of life, including how one regards oneself (levels of self-esteem, emotional outlook, self-care, resilience, etc.) and how one regards others (interpersonal relationships, expressions of behaviour, and so on).

In a nutshell... Parenting peril 1

- *Some children take on a nurturing role, comforting and supporting their parents through grief.*
- *To their own detriment, the children hide their pain and 'act strong' in order not to upset their parents further.*
- *If this is happening, parents can opt to cry when their children are not nearby to see it.*

Parenting peril 2: when children grow up too fast and become 'mini adults'

Some children (typically the eldest sibling) might feel that they are expected to step into a parental role (often the role of the parent who is no longer living in the house) and share parental responsibilities and decision making, and caring for younger siblings. At times, this may seem unavoidable to a parent, who now has to make decisions on their own, and has no one with whom to share household duties and tasks.

Parents need to be mindful of their children's ages and their stages of development. Even children who appear older than they are, and are responsible and capable, are still *children* despite the way they may look or act. Parents might think that children are coping with the added responsibilities, when internally the children are actually distressed or overwhelmed by the tasks assigned to them. Anxiety about disappointing a parent, or being seen as unhelpful, could prevent children from displaying the stress they might be feeling. All children want their parents' approval and this could act as a big incentive to encourage them to try harder to please their parents - even if they are not really coping with the demands placed on them.

If you are relying on your children for more help and assistance following your family's separation, consider their ages and give them small tasks that they can realistically manage. This will help them to feel good about their contribution and give them a sense of accomplishment. When children fail at a task or don't do as well as their parents expected, this can affect their self-esteem.

In turn, they might put pressure on themselves to be 'perfect' in their attempts to achieve unmanageable tasks.

As much as possible, invite other adults (family, extended family, neighbours, friends, even local volunteers) to assist you. This will allow your children to focus on their grief and process the changes they are experiencing. Similarly, it is important that children are allowed to be just children. There will be plenty of time in their adult lives for them to do 'adult' things, and when they will have to cope with adult anxieties and worry about looking after their own children.

In a nutshell... Parenting peril 2

- *Relying on children to share parental responsibilities places stress on children.*
- *Parents might think children are coping with added responsibilities, when internally the children are overwhelmed by them.*
- *If you are relying on your children for more help following separation, consider their age and give them small tasks they can realistically manage.*
- *As much as possible, invite other adults to help and assist you*

Parenting peril 3: when children place parents' needs before their own

Children can become very protective of their parents following family separation. This is evident, for example, when they sacrifice their own needs in favour of the interests of their parents. For instance, a child might perceive that living predominantly with one parent will leave the other parent feeling sad or alone. Consequently, the child informs her parents that she wishes to start spending alternate nights at each parent's home. Or in another instance, a child might be aware of his parents' concerns about finances following separation. He feigns disinterest in order to avoid attending the sporting event he had been looking forward to, thereby sparing his parents the expense associated with attending. These examples, however impractical, unfair and potentially detrimental to the child's own stability, routine and happiness, are common displays of the nurturing instinct of children during times of family stress.

This sacrificing behaviour on the part of children is another instance of a 'peril' of which parents need to be conscious following separation. It can take many forms and can motivate what children say and do, as well as the general behaviour they display. Professionals who work with families in post-separation negotiations and counselling are trained to expertly explore the actions and input provided by children. They recognise that children might not be acting in accordance with their own wants and needs. Parents, however, might not recognise this underlying motivating behaviour and could too readily accept what children say or do.

Asking further questions of children can help parents and professionals determine the reasoning behind children's statements and behaviours. Children can then be encouraged to voice opinions and act in ways that are more true to and in line with their *own* needs.

In a nutshell... Parenting peril 3

- *Children often sacrifice their own needs following family separation, in an attempt to protect their parents from feeling sad or alone.*
- *Ask questions to determine the reasoning behind children's behaviour, and encourage them to act in ways more in line with their own needs*

Parenting peril 4: when children are on 'look-out'

When your children return from a visit to their other parent, allow them to share the information they want to disclose about it. It is important to avoid asking a lot of questions about either their visit or your ex-partner. This can lead to children feeling as though they are being 'interrogated' and that they must tell you everything, and can increase their levels of stress. It can also backfire very quickly, because it teaches them to shut down and tell you nothing. No one feels like sharing if they are being interrogated.

Just let your children share what they want to share, and ask a few general questions, such as 'How was your visit? You can tell me a bit about it, if you like.' Asking questions like this lets children know that you are interested and open to them talking about their other parent. It also gives them permission to decide how much they want to share, or whether they want to share anything at all. This provides them with options and a sense of personal power. Therefore respect your children's right to share information with you, but also their right to privacy. They are not obliged to tell you details of their visit, or bring you up to date on any changes in your ex-partner's life. Questions you might have about your ex-partner are a matter for you alone.

Also be aware that sometimes children choose not to talk about their visit, in order not to upset their parent in their time of grief. If your children had a fantastic visit, telling you about it could distress you - children are quite insightful and protective of their parents during separation!

In a nutshell... Parenting peril 4

- *Following a child's visit to their other parent, ask a few general questions; this tells children they can talk about their other parent, but also gives them permission not to.*
- *Avoid placing pressure on children by asking a lot of questions about either their visit or your ex-partner.*
- *Sometimes children choose not to talk about their visit; this is especially the case if they had an enjoyable time with their other parent.*

Parenting peril 5: when children become the 'fall guy'

There is a significant power imbalance between children and adults. Adults not only are physically larger, but their mental and emotional processes are better developed. Sometimes, parents will direct their grief feelings of anger, sadness, confusion, anxiety and pain at their children, simply because 'they're there'.

No parent consciously decides to 'dump' their feelings on to their children, thus using them as a 'fall guy' or 'scapegoat', but it does happen. There are two main reasons for this (neither of which justifies it, of course!).

One reason is that the parent is not addressing their grief, telling themselves that they are 'fine'. They bottle up their feelings until they can no longer keep them hidden, and suddenly explode. A second reason is that the parent, attempting to come to terms with their own grief, projects on to their child the anger they feel towards their ex-partner. This may be because the child resembles the ex-partner, or because the ex-partner either is not there to take the force of the anger, or refuses to take it. In both instances, the explosion of feelings is directed at the child, who, because of the power imbalance, usually has little option but to absorb it.

For some parents, therefore, 'dumping' feelings on to children in this manner, however unconsciously, is a 'safe' and 'easy' way of ridding themselves of pent- up emotions, because children are unable to assert or distance themselves in the way that adults can. But 'dumping' emotions in this way is a display of *unhealthy anger*, as described in stage 7 of the grief cycle in Chapter 1.

In a nutshell... Parenting peril 5

- *Sometimes, parents will direct their grief feelings at their children, simply because the children are 'there'.*
- *The power imbalance between adults and children means that children usually have little option but to absorb their parent's grief.*
- *'Dumping' emotions in this way is a display of unhealthy anger.*

Parenting peril 6: when children are treated as a 'go-between'

It is not uncommon for parents to find it difficult to communicate with each other following separation. The emotions and grief are raw. Although both parents will attempt to keep their exchanges 'civil' and 'adult', it is common for hurt feelings and unresolved issues to get in the way. It can take years to arrive at a point where communication between ex-partners can occur relatively smoothly. In the meantime, some parents find it easier to relay information via their children.

This is another 'peril' of which parents need to be mindful. It is a stressful and inappropriate task for children. Not only does it make them responsible for remembering to relay the message, but they also have to remember what the message actually is: a more difficult task for children than for adults. Additionally, it also means that children are responsible for receiving and dealing with an ex-partner's reaction to the message, which might not be positive.

Children need their energy to come to terms with the separation and the changes taking place within and around them, and to work through their grief. Don't be tempted to ask them to take on the role of 'go-between'. It is simply too big a responsibility for children, whatever their age.

If you and your ex-partner have difficulty communicating with each other, the following strategy for trying to improve this might help. Begin by agreeing on the easy things first.

When arguments start, stop and walk away. Stick to the topic: avoid tangents and talking about past issues. If there are valid reasons why you are unable to pass messages to your ex-partner yourself, send them in a letter or an email, or ask another adult if they will agree to act as a 'go- between' for you.

In a nutshell... Parenting peril 6

- *It is not uncommon for parents to find it difficult to communicate with each other following separation.*
- *Sending messages to an ex-partner via children is a stressful and inappropriate task for children; alternative ways should be sought.*

Parenting peril 7: when children become an image of your ex-partner

One or more children might strongly resemble your ex-partner, in appearance, mannerisms, or other ways. To a grieving parent, any memories of an ex-partner can trigger a grief response. Be mindful that although your child might resemble your ex-partner, they *are not* your ex-partner.

Keep your responses to your children positive and supportive. Avoid statements such as: 'You're just like your father' or 'Every time I look at you, I see your mother.' It is unfair to children if parents project on to them their own feelings of grief or any issues they may have concerning their ex-partner.

In a nutshell... Parenting peril 7

- *Although children might resemble an ex-partner, they are not that ex-partner.*
- *Keep responses to children positive and supportive; avoid statements such as: 'You're just like your father' or 'Every time I look at you, I see your mother.'*

Parenting peril 8: when children are set up as friend or foe

Remember that your ex-partner is 'Mum' or 'Dad' to your children. There may be unresolved issues between you and your ex-partner, but as just mentioned in relation to 'Parenting peril 7', it is important to avoid complaining about them, discrediting them, calling them names or speaking disrespectfully about them in front of your children. To do so places children in a very difficult position.

Children love their parents and want to look up to and respect them. They need to know that they are loved by both parents and that in turn they are allowed to continue loving both. This is especially the case during family separation. Separation leaves families exposed, and children feeling scared and vulnerable. They need to know that it is all right for them to feel love for and look up to both parents, and to be able to talk about and have contact with them.

In a nutshell... Parenting peril 8

- *A parent should avoid speaking badly about their children's other parent.*
- *Separation leaves families exposed and children feeling vulnerable; they need to know they are loved by both parents and that they can continue loving both.*

Parenting peril 9: when children act as grief counsellors

Sometimes parents may slide into a pattern of talking through their grief with their children. This usually starts as small measured exchanges or 'chats', but roles can quickly become blurred. The child is no longer seen as a child, but as an 'on-call' counsellor, ready to lend an ear whenever the parent needs to 'talk'. This can result in a situation where the parent freely discloses their feelings of grief, personal fears or stressors and, essentially, pours out their soul.

If this has happened to you, it is wonderful that you are willing to talk about your feelings. However, rather than talking to your children about them, you might be encouraged to find a counsellor, a friend, a relative, a neighbour or some other adult you trust, and relate your pain and hurt feelings to them. They are a more appropriate support to you than your children. Your job as a parent is to listen to your children's grief and help them through it — not the other way round!

In a nutshell... Parenting peril 9

- *Parents may slide into a pattern of talking about their feelings to their children.*
- *This is an inappropriate role for children: parents should turn instead to a counsellor, friend or relative, or another adult they trust.*

Parenting peril 10: when boys become the 'man of the house'

Many mothers observe periods following separation when usually their eldest son steps into the role of 'man of the house'. Typical behaviour exhibited by boys who do this includes: telling their younger siblings what to do; setting boundaries for them; firmly telling them off for not adhering to these limits and fighting with them; reassuring their mother; protecting her and bossing her around; displaying exaggerated 'masculine' behaviour and mimicking their father or other older male role models.

If you have a son and this happens to you, tell him that he is *your son* and that he isn't expected to take on the role of father or husband. He is probably attempting to help and comfort you, but if the behaviour goes unmonitored and unaddressed, it may lead to many problems for the boy (concerning issues of power or control, for example, or developmental problems). Furthermore, although your son may mean well, such behaviour is not a healthy coping strategy: it is likely that he is using it as a way of avoiding or minimising his grief.

In a nutshell... Parenting peril 10

- *Many mothers observe periods following separation when their son steps into the role of 'man of the house'.*
- *Although probably trying to help and comfort their mother, boys should be told that they are not expected to take on the role of father or husband.*
- *However well meant, such behaviour is not a healthy coping strategy; if not stopped, it can lead to problems later.*

Parenting peril 11: when children are treated as friends or 'buddies'

It is important to recognise that your children rely on you to provide two equally important things: nurturing and structure. Structure refers to routines, boundaries, rules and predictability. Sometimes following separation, parents focus so much on nurturing their children, they forget about structure. The result is children who are overindulged!

One way in which parents overindulge their children is by attempting to become their children's friend or 'buddy' rather than their parent. This can be seen when parents buy children gifts in addition to those they would normally have bought them; take them on more trips than they would usually have taken them on; allow them to do as they wish, stay up late, eat 'junk' food and break rules; and talk to them as they would to an adult friend.

What is important is a parent's relationship with their children. You are your children's *parent*, and spoiling them won't compensate for the separation, or gain you any greater standing in their eyes. Neither, in the long run, will it spare your children from grief or make you their 'friend'.

In a nutshell... Parenting peril 11

- *Following separation, parents may focus too much on nurturing and not enough on structure, resulting in children who are overindulged.*
- *Overindulging children will not compensate for the separation, or spare children from grief.*
- *More important is a parent's relationship with their children.*

Summary

All eleven scenarios described in this section are *maladaptive* coping strategies. They are neither healthy nor effective. They might produce some short-term gains or benefits, but they also impose on the grief process, on healing and on children's ability to develop fully or appropriately. Furthermore, they can do permanent damage to relationships between children and parents.

Parents or children who are engaging in any of these strategies would be strongly advised to change them. If this applies to you, you don't need to berate yourself for adopting such strategies. Separation places families under extreme stress, and gives rise to emotional distress and feelings of vulnerability and fear. The coping strategies described emerge as ways of coping with these feelings, but they are neither positive nor helpful. Allow yourself to step out of such patterns of behaviour and acknowledge that you and your children are doing your best.

Common reactions of children to separation

Just as adults grieve in individual and unique ways, so too do children. One child might display all the indicators mentioned for their age group, whereas another may show signs of only a few. Some children will pass through phases briefly, others will take longer.

Being informed about children's reactions is important for parents. It allows them to interpret their children's reactions within the context of *grief*; that is, as a *demonstration* of grief. In doing so, it enables them to respond to their children's grief, rather than just to the reaction itself or to a particular behaviour. For example, think about the common scenario of children whose school performance drops following separation. Their grief affects their energy levels, concentration and emotions. They are preoccupied with thoughts of separation and want space in which to process what is happening to their family. They feel confused by their feelings. They have new needs.

Attributing the drop in school performance to grief will alter the approach parents take in addressing the issue. Instead of arranging for a private tutor in order to help boost grades, for instance, they are more likely in the first instance to ask their children about their feelings. They will invite them to talk about their needs, will offer reassurance and will be conscious of the effects of change on them. They will listen to and support their children, and address their grief. Only after they have done all this might they also decide to call in a tutor.

0-3 years of age

Children in this age group are learning to trust and form attachments to their parents. In order to do this, they need many things from their parents, including consistency. Changes to routines and environment brought on by family separation are likely to impact on them greatly. Infants see themselves as an extension of their parent(s) because they have not yet developed a sense of themselves as an individual, and hence will be confused and unsettled by the absence of their parent. Similarly, young children won't understand what is happening and may search for their absent parent or try to cling to the parent who is available. The stress they experience internally is likely to be evident in behavioural changes, such as crying, or changes to sleeping and eating patterns. Parents can help their young child by looking for ways to keep as many routines as consistent as possible. Providing increased attention, affection and quality time can be helpful in responding to their underlying fears of abandonment and uncertainty.

3-6 years of age

Children in this age group begin to develop independent thought and to become aware of themselves as individuals. In the process of developing these skills, as noted earlier, they often form rigid 'black and white' points of view and struggle to understand 'grey shades' of life. To find explanations and solutions to their changing family, young children often engage in make-believe games, in which they can 'control' outcomes. Because this age group is egocentric, children are likely to believe they have more 'power' in events that take place than they actually do and, for this reason, will also feel 'responsibility' and 'blame' for what has happened in their family. Their fears and uncertainty could result in their reverting back to younger developmental behaviours, such as bedwetting, separation anxiety or 'baby talk'. They are likely to ask lots of questions repeatedly, yet struggle to understand parents' explanations for separation. Parents need to keep responses to children's questions simple and consistent. It would also be helpful to tell children that the decision to separate was made by the parents and that the children are not responsible. Reassure them that they will not be abandoned, and that you love them and will take care of them always.

6-12 years of age

Children in this age group learn about and identify with structures outside of their family unit, such as friendship circles, school communities and sporting groups. They will want to belong to and feel accepted by these groups and will feel fearful of anything that threatens to expose them as 'different' from others in the group. They might therefore seek to hide their family separation by disengaging from some activities, or masking their emotions and acting 'fine' or 'grown-up'. Parents need to be sensitive to children's fears of being viewed as 'different' from their peers, by being flexible and reassuring children that they are loved, accepted and safe. Likewise, any displays on the part of children, of 'parenting' their siblings or parents, of workaholism and overachieving, or of siding with one parent in conflicts, need to be addressed so that parent and child boundaries are clear.

Children might also fluctuate between feeling hostile and feeling empathetic towards their parents. Children's grief feelings can include worries of being abandoned and might be expressed through behaviour that includes displays of aggression, withdrawal, or reverting to younger developmental behaviours (such as tantrums, separation anxiety or wanting to sleep in their parent's bed). Although children will understand most explanations offered by parents, they will feel emotionally 'stuck' and confused at the same time. While working through their grief feelings, they could show a decline in school performance, concentration, energy and interest in hobbies. Parents are advised to provide opportunities for discussion that encourage children to verbalise their thoughts and feelings, rather than expressing them through their behaviour.

12 years +

Children and young people in this age group build further on their independence, personal identity and autonomy. They often do this by fluctuating between feeling 'independent' and feeling 'dependent' on parents. They will identify strongly with their friends and are more likely to turn to them for support and someone to confide in about their changing family and their grief feelings. At times they are likely to feel isolated and misunderstood, and they will often display their sadness and confusion through anger, rebellion, depression or withdrawal. Parents need to be firm but flexible and to give their teenage children space and privacy while simultaneously providing clear boundaries. They also need to 'be there' for their teenagers when the pendulum swings back towards the 'dependent' end of the spectrum, providing love, comfort and support to help them process their confusion.

Keeping the channels of communication open will encourage teenagers to turn to parents for talks when they choose to. Showing an interest in teenagers' activities and opinions, and providing opportunities for them to make some independent decisions about family separation, will allow them to exercise some personal power. This will also help them build their self-esteem and will demonstrate parental acceptance of their independence and 'growing up'. Keep the boundaries and rules for teenagers consistent and in place. Where possible, provide some opportunities for them to engage in one-to-one quality time with each parent, so that they can also feel independent of their siblings.

(Developmental stages adapted in part from Illsley Clarke and Dawson, 1998.)

In a nutshell... Children's reactions to separation

- *Children, like adults, grieve in individual and unique ways. They might display all or only a few of the indicators listed for their age group.*
- *Parents need to be informed about children's reactions to separation, to enable them to interpret these within the context of grief.*
- *A decline in school performance might indicate that children are preoccupied with thoughts of their parents' separation.*

Possible signs of difficulty adjusting

Some indicators that children could be experiencing difficulty adjusting to their parents' separation are listed below. Many of these will vary according to the age of children and their emotional and physical development. (For more information about further strategies to support their children, parents might speak to a therapist who specialises in post-separation counselling and child counselling.) Indicators include:

- Decline in school grades
- Poor concentration
- Aggression
- Being bullied
- Misbehaviour at school
- Low self-esteem
- Reverting to younger behaviour (for example, toilet-trained children may wet themselves; baby talk; thumb sucking)
- Nightmares
- Withdrawing into themselves and distancing themselves from others

- Being overly clingy towards parents
- Controlling and dominating others (including parents, other adults)
- Being passive and unsure
- Attention seeking
- Seeking comfort and reassurance constantly
- Feeling tired and drained
- Loss of motivation
- Defiance and rebellion
- Difficulty in maintaining friendships or heavy dependence on others
- Wanting to sleep in same room or bed as parent
- Fear of the dark, or other phobias
- Violent outbursts (biting, hitting, smacking other children)
- Increase in sensitivity (for example, more tearful and moody).

Some of the indicators listed may be experienced briefly by children immediately following separation; in some children, however, they may persist and therefore become more of a concern for parents.

Children will sometimes choose to express their feelings through their behaviour. Therefore, underlying many of the indicators, or *behaviours*, listed above are *feelings* of grief, pain, fear and confusion. Children are communicating their *need* for love, attention, reassurance, stability and comfort.

Parents can help their children by realising that many children will display one or more of the above behaviours during separation. Talking with children about the separation and inviting them to tell you about their fears and concerns can help. It can open the way for children to move from communicating through their behaviour towards communicating verbally.

Discussions can provide you with information about the general and specific concerns children have, enabling you to reassure them and find ways to address these concerns. Maintaining as many routines as possible for children will also help: structure and routine provide predictability and therefore a sense of safety.

In a nutshell... Difficulty adjusting

- *Indicators that children could be experiencing difficulty adjusting to separation vary, depending on their age and their emotional and physical development.*
- *Children often express their feelings through their behaviour.*
- *By doing so, children are attempting to communicate their need for love, attention, reassurance, stability and comfort.*

Explaining separation to children

Explaining separation to children is not easy. It is emotionally difficult for parents to tell their children that their family is going to change. How do you explain to a young child, who sees things in 'black and white', that you are still going to be a family, but that the family - *their* family - will be different? They will take the changes to their family personally: it is, after all, their family. Even older children will not understand how this can happen *to them* — how such a personal thing can happen without their agreement. They will struggle to understand that such a thing is out of their control, that it can happen without their permission.

The changes will be significant. They will hurt, sadden and confuse children, and children are unlikely to take them 'in their stride'. They will resist them. They will feel vulnerable and fear further change: they will want their family to stay together.

There is no universal explanation that parents can offer to their children: no clear 'right way' of telling them. However, the following guidelines might help.

- Prepare in advance when you will tell your children and who will be there. Will you and your ex-partner tell them together, or will you each tell them separately? Where will you tell them?

- Consider whether you will tell all your children at the same time, or individually. If there is a significant age difference between them, it might be better to tell them individually. An older child will want more detail and explanation than a younger one.
- Prepare in advance what you are going to say. Also be aware of what you will not disclose, because some information is not appropriate for a child to know. Practise your explanation.
- Find a time when you will not be disturbed. Allow time for discussion and questions.
- Keep explanations age appropriate. Information given to younger children will need to be brief and 'to the point'. Young children have shorter attention spans and will need to have information explained to them more than once. They will not understand vague or 'grey' definitions. Stick to facts: explain what will happen, where, when and how, and who will be involved.
- Use words your children will understand. Speak slowly and clearly. Pause intermittently to allow them to absorb what you are saying. Avoid rushing what you want to say because you want

to get it 'over and done with' quickly.

- Keep it simple. Avoid long explanations and telling children too many of the details about what happened, or about what could happen. Be honest, but recognise that what your children need most is to know that things will be stable - they don't need to know how this will be achieved.
- Don't give false hope. In other words, don't tell children that reconciliation is possible if this isn't the case. To do so prolongs their denial and fantasy and invites wishful thinking.
- Don't make any promises. Instead, tell your children that you will do your best to meet their needs. Invite them to keep you informed of how they feel and what they need from you.
- Allow children to ask questions. Ask them what questions they have for you and what they need from you now. Tell them that they can ask you further questions as they think of them.
- Expect emotional grief reactions, including anger, fear and denial. Your 'talk' together is unlikely to be a calm one.
- Be prepared for a series of discussions. Children need to know the door is open and that the

separation can be discussed again whenever they need to.

- Children might feel overwhelmed and, initially, be able to register only a small amount of information. Ask them to repeat what they have understood.

- Reassure children that they are not to blame. Make it clear that the problems are between you and your ex-partner, and that although the separation is 'happening' to the children too, they did nothing to cause it. Be willing to repeat this truth over and over again.

- Have a sense of what your children will want to know from you. Some common things include: wanting to know that they are still loved and will continue to see both parents; where they will live; whether they will continue to go to the same school; where the parent who will no longer be living with the family will now live, and how to contact that parent.

- Realise that children are likely to feel abandoned and might fear losing the parent with whom they are now to live as well as the parent who is leaving. They need to know what they can expect in terms of stability and ongoing contact with both parents. Address these fears of abandonment. Children might not voice their fears, but they are likely to experience them internally. They need to know that both parents will be there for them. (To children, their family is their world and they rely on it almost exclusively for all their needs. The fear children have is that if one parent leaves, the other might too. They fear being left alone to fend for themselves. Separation turns their family - and therefore their world - upside down. They need stability and reassurance in order to feel safe and loved.)

- Notice your children's reactions and pay attention to their body language - use these as cues to assess their levels of distress, and to guide you in what you are saying and how you are saying it. Slow down if they look overwhelmed, and pause if you have 'lost them' or they look confused.

- Adjust your own body language accordingly. You might sit or lean in closer to them, or rest a hand over theirs. Alternatively, you might sit back, break eye contact or be very still if you sense that they want some space from you.

- Hug and comfort the children if they will let you. Give them space if they storm out and want to be alone, and then follow up with them later. All children need reassurance at this time, even if they respond with anger. Don't force them to sit there and listen. They might be too overwhelmed to take in any more information than they have already heard. Let them walk away, and be willing to continue the conversation at a later time.

- Keep explanations consistent. Don't offer one explanation one day and a different one on another. Be clear and keep all information and plans consistent. Children need to know that although you might not have all the answers at this time, what you say is honest and can be relied upon. They need to know they can count on you and on what you tell them.

- Finally, and importantly, don't discredit what your children tell you, because this invites them to 'shut down' and keep things to themselves. Avoid telling them how they should or should not feel or think, or what they should or should not want. Just listen without judging them and accept what they say. They don't have to make sense or be logical - they are children and are grieving. They will see things differently from you. Be glad that they are communicating with you. Your job is to keep the door of communication open, and to be supportive and accessible. Think about what they would like you to say. If you were in their shoes, what would you want your parent to say?

Avoid saying:

- 'That's ridiculous. You shouldn't think that.'
- 'That's silly.'
- 'Nobody feels like that.'
- 'That's a stupid suggestion.'
- 'It's a waste of time getting caught up in those thoughts.'
- 'The problem with you is ...'
- 'You're imagining things.'
- 'You're going on and on.'
- 'Why can't you just get over it?'
- 'Don't talk about it.'
- 'I don't want to know about it.'
- 'You should just let go and stop worrying yourself about it.'
- 'Why do you keep bringing it up?'
- 'That's a stupid thought.'
- 'You're worrying yourself over nothing.'

Do say:

- 'I'm pleased you told me.'
- 'I'm glad you are honest with me.'
- 'I understand.'
- 'It took courage for you to say that.'
- 'You look upset and confused. I'm glad you are showing me how you feel.'
- 'What do you need from me?'
- 'I feel confused sometimes too.'
- 'It's okay to feel that way/think those thoughts.'
- 'It's normal to think that. It will take time. Keep talking to me.'
- 'I'm here for you. I love you.'

Summary

Flexibility is key. The style of explanation you use with one child might not work with another. Similarly, you might need to explain the separation to the same child in more than one way, just as you might need to repeat information over again. You may also need to give information in instalments: your children might be unwilling to hear it all at once.

However, some things are certain. Your children need to know they are loved and that, in turn, they can still love both you and your ex-partner. They need to know that both of you will be there for them: that they will not be abandoned.

They need stability and predictability from you, and to know that they can continue seeing both of you. They need to have ready access to you both and to know how to contact you. They also need to know that they are not to blame for the separation, that nothing they did caused it, and that nothing will change it.

Finally, in explaining the process of separation to children, you might find it helpful to draw on the information given in this book to guide you. You may also like to make use of the other books in this series. You can read the illustrated *My Mum and*

Dad are Separating, Children's Book to younger children, or give them the children's book to read themselves if they are old enough to do so on their own. Children aged between 5 and 13 may like to try the activities in the *My Mum and Dad are Separating, Activity Book* for Children.

The potential long-term effects of separation on both adults and children

Adults and children will process grief and family separation differently. Therefore, the potential long-term effects of separation on adults and children will also be different. While an adult is grieving over the loss of their family as they knew it before the separation, they can expect to feel the impact of their grief in extremely painful ways. Gradually, however, adults are likely to process and work through their grief, and to find that the intensity of their initial response lessens. Eventually, the separation may simply fade into a memory. Healing will have taken place; they will have recovered and will be ready to move on with their lives. Adults are able to adjust to such a major life-changing event because they have developed the skills and internal coping processes necessary to do so. A similar event experienced in childhood will have a different impact and different consequences.

Childhood is a brief but significant stage in life. The pathways in children's brains are still forming, and their internal belief systems and view of themselves and their world are still being shaped. Similarly, their mental, emotional and psychological processes are still developing. Because these important building blocks for the future are not yet fully formed, the impact and consequences of family separation are likely to be more long lasting.

Children thrive best in environments that provide support and stability, safety and structure, caring and affection, and togetherness and belonging. They need these things regardless of whether they belong to 'intact' families or 'separated' families. How well their needs are met, in either family context, largely determines how they develop and function emotionally and psychologically.

Adults can usually rely on their own emotional, mental and psychological resources to help them cope with grief and separation. Children, however, need parents and other caring adults to help them process their grief and accept the separation of their family. We can think of this in terms of a 'road map'. Whereas an adult's resources might be fully mapped, those of children resemble a map in the making - not all the roads have yet been built and the map is therefore incomplete. Children need help with understanding what is happening, and to be given strategies for coping.

Without this kind of support, children's levels of stress and anxiety might rise significantly, leading them to try to help themselves. Their attempts to build their own roads on the map, using the limited skills they have, are likely to be ineffective and maladaptive. The strategies a child learns in childhood are often carried over into adulthood, which means that when roads are built, they tend to be long lasting. This is why it is so important that children learn 'healthy' methods of coping and receive adequate support to process their grief and adjust to change. Parents will need to help children to move through the 'map' of their grief and to guide them appropriately.

Parents are encouraged to provide love, support, care, safety, stability, nurturing and structure, as these things will be very important to a grieving child. 'Being there' for children, and helping them through the range of emotions they will experience, is very important. Answering questions, providing information and giving reassurance where you can means a lot in the life of any child, but especially to a child who is grieving. It will help the child to heal and adjust, and to develop fully and appropriately.

Without this support, children may not manage to integrate the changes effectively. Instead, they may become trapped in the maladaptive coping strategies they develop in an attempt to cope as best they can. With such support, however, they are much more likely to develop to their full emotional, mental and psychological capacity - and into well-balanced adults with healthy levels of functioning. Like all children, they will look to their parents or other caring adults to meet their developmental needs and to help them to thrive and prosper.

In a nutshell... The potential long-term effects of separation

- *The potential long-term effects of separation are likely to be greater for children than for adults, and could impact on them far into the future.*
- *Children's mental, emotional and psychological processes are still developing; they therefore require support to help them through the stress and grief they are experiencing.*
- *How well children process grief and family separation depends greatly on the external support available to them.*
- *Providing love, support, care, safety, stability, nurturing and structure is very important in helping a grieving child to heal, adjust and develop.*

Parental guilt

A multitude of guilt themes have been voiced by parents who are separating or have separated. This section addresses four very common themes. Parents might relate to some or all of these, which may be experienced in varying degrees and for different lengths of time.

Parental guilt 1: your personal best is all you can do

'I could have ...', I should have ...' Although guilt is a normal part of the grieving process, there comes a time when you need to put it to rest and acknowledge that you did your best and are doing your best now. No one can do more than their personal best, and comparing yourself with others will not help you recognise *your* personal best.

As each of us learns and develops, we gain skills that enable us to do things differently. The person we will be in the future might do things very differently from the way we do them now. But you are not the 'you' of the future and you cannot apply the hindsight you will have in the future to your present situation. All you can do is draw on your unique talents, perceptions, gifts and strengths to get you through the 'now'.

It can be hard to accept that even when you do your best, separation can still occur. Millions of parents have done their best in their marriages and as parents to their children, yet still separation has ensued. It may not seem 'fair'. But, as we all know, unfair life events do occur. People cannot control everything that happens to them, but they can use their skills to do their best. That is all you can ask of yourself.

In a nutshell... Parental guilt 1

- *No one can do more than their personal best.*
- *All you can do is draw on your unique attributes to get you through your present situation.*
- *Even when you do your best, separation can occur.*

Parental guilt 2: the vice - to work or stay home with the children

Separation invariably brings with it a myriad of changes that impact on the family. One such change involves work. Some previously full-time, 'stay-at- home' parents are forced to join the workforce, as a result of financial burdens created by separation. Others take on second or third jobs. In some families, however, finances improve and parents might opt to reduce the hours they work, or leave paid employment altogether.

Both women and men have the right to decide their personal work/home ratio. Following separation, many working mothers (in particular) feel guilty about choosing to work and pursue a career, but there is no need for them to feel this way. Parents of both gender love their children and have unique parenting skills and strengths. They also have professional ambitions, and a wish to contribute to society through the workplace. Millions of people worldwide fit into this category. They are loving, involved and effective parents, who also happen to work. They have opted to balance family life with their profession.

Working parents and parents who stay at home contribute to their families and society in unique and equally important ways. It is important to recognise the strengths of both and to see the positive opportunities that each offers for acting as a positive role model for children.

You can work and bring up children without judging, condemning or undervaluing yourself. You also have the right to have your decision respected by others.

In a nutshell... Parental guilt 2

- *Whether to work or stay at home following separation is often determined by financial status.*
- *Working parents and those who stay at home contribute to their families and society in unique and equally important ways.*
- *Each provides opportunities for acting as a positive role model for children.*

Parental guilt 3: what about the children?

No parent sets out wanting to separate. It is usually the last resort, when all else has been tried and has failed. Yet even so, it can be common for parents to periodically question whether it might have been better, for the children, if the family had remained together as a 'nuclear family.' But there is a difference between questioning this point and agonising over it. Naturally, parents would prefer not to subject their children to family separation. However, continually questioning the decisions that have been made and the circumstances your family is now in is likely to prolong the 'guilt' stage of grief and prevent a healthy progression through grief and change.

As we have seen, separation affects children. But berating yourself about family separation won't spare your children from their own grief feelings, or facilitate your own healing. Continued guilt feelings are more likely to keep you stuck in the past, draining you of the mental and emotional resources you need in order to provide effective support to your children now. Allow yourself to move through grief in a manner that is gentler and kinder to yourself, by accepting that from within your present situation you can do things that will impact positively on and shape your children.

It is important to remember that, as mentioned in the previous section, how well children recover from family separation, and how well they process their grief, is determined by many factors, including parental support and stability, safety and structure, caring and affection, and togetherness and belonging. Children of both 'intact' and 'separated' families require these things for their emotional and psychological development. It is the aim of this book to make it easier for parents, families and therapists to support a grieving child, to help them to process their grief in healthy ways, and to have their important developmental needs met.

In a nutshell... Parental guilt 3

- *Separation is usually the last resort, but parents may still question whether it would have been better, for the children, if the family had remained together.*
- *However, continued guilt feelings will hinder a parent's ability to provide the effective support children need.*
- *Children process their grief best in environments that provide support and stability.*

Parental guilt 4: am I making the right choices?

Parents don't have to force themselves to make too many decisions at once. Nor do they need to berate themselves for not making the 'best' decisions. You can allow time for yourself and your family to adjust to one set of changes before considering others. It is unwise to make too many major changes or decisions immediately following separation, because the raw emotions of grief cloud clear thinking. Most people won't be able to feel and think at the same time: their feelings will always come first. Hence, hasty or rash decisions made at a time of grief might be regretted when emotions have settled down a little.

Parents can sometimes have unrealistic expectations of themselves and then feel guilty when they don't live up to these. Pressuring yourself to 'get things *right*' and 'make the *best* decisions' is likely to prevent you from moving on from the guilt phase of grief. Engaging in this behaviour could actually hinder your problem-solving abilities, rather than improve them. If you do notice yourself falling into the 'guilt' trap of criticising yourself for the decisions you are making, perhaps lower your expectations and avoid thinking that there are 'perfect solutions'. Where possible, wait until you feel clear about the decisions you are making and then move forward with them confidently and intentionally.

In a nutshell... Parental guilt 4

- *Avoid making too many decisions too soon: allow time for yourself and your family to adjust to one set of changes before considering others.*
- *Hasty decisions made in the early stages of grief might be regretted later.*
- *Wait until you feel clear about your decisions, then move forward with them confidently.*

Summary

Guilt is a normal part of the process of grief. It will often be put aside for a while, but then revisited. Anything can act as a trigger to bring on another bout of guilt and, while it lasts, people often feel vulnerable and low.

There is a difference between experiencing guilt as a step in the grief process, and being trapped by it. Some people become incapacitated by guilt, and continue to berate themselves for years following separation and divorce. They use their guilt as a psychological 'whip' with which to punish themselves and allow no space for healing or acceptance. They find they are unable to adapt.

If you are in this situation, you might find it helpful to look forward 10 or 20 years, to a time when your children have grown up. Imagine they are looking back to the time of separation. What might their memories of the separation be? How might they remember you? How would you like them to remember you? And what is the difference between the two? What would you like them to know?

When all is said and done, people keep moving forward. Every day people's lives are marked by change, tragedy, pain, surprise and an opportunity to step into something new. From these events emerge qualities of resilience, strength, understanding and compassion for others.

When life strikes an all-powerful blow, it is difficult to imagine that it can get better. It is hard to believe that anything will ever feel all right again. However, all over the world, people find themselves taking first one step forward and then another. These steps we take are small and appear insignificant, but their accumulation determines our destination. The qualities we develop on the way are testament to our journey. They mark who we are, who we become and how we will be remembered.

Put guilt in its place: as a temporary 'stop'. Don't make it your permanent 'home'. It is not your destination!

Chapter 3

Reframing Family

Tips for making access changeover times easier

Changeover times can be very disruptive for children, even when parents are civil to one another and there is little conflict between them. Children need time to prepare themselves to leave the home of one parent, and time to adjust to staying with the other.

It is especially trying for children and parents if children are engaged in activities they are enjoying and don't want to be interrupted or taken away from them (watching a programme on television, for example, or playing an interesting game). Giving children plenty of notice and preparing them for the other parent's arrival will help them to start 'winding down' and finishing off activities, so that they are ready to leave with their other parent.

The period of time required for children to adjust from living with one parent to staying with the other can be considerable. To understand this, it can be helpful to liken it to driving a car through different conditions. For example, when you have been travelling down a main road for a while and turn on to an unmade track, do you continue to drive at the same speed? Of course not. You slow down, steer to avoid potholes, brake more frequently and generally pay closer attention to the road, until you ease into it. Moving between households, and from one parent to another, is rather like this for children. It takes time for them to ease into it.

Therefore, expect some disruption and a period of adjustment when children are preparing to leave or return to your care. Different homes have different rules, structure, routines, atmosphere and, invariably, parenting styles. Children need time to adjust not only from one 'system' to the other, but also mentally and emotionally. They will share a different bond and have a different relationship with each parent: they need time to 'disconnect' from one parent and 'reattach' to the other. Children will rarely adjust automatically, and it is therefore important not to minimise the time needed for this.

Given below are some suggestions to help your family manage changeover times more effectively. They refer specifically to low-, moderate- and high- conflict situations. It usually takes time for parents to find the best method of changeover for their children. You might find the answer here, or you might create a method of your own, based on your children's temperaments, needs and stages of grief. Allow time to try a method and allow for trial and error. You might have to experiment with many variations before you decide on one that works best for your children.

In a nutshell... Tips for easier access changeover times

- *When children are preparing to leave or return to your care, expect some disruption.*
- *Children need time to adjust not only between one home 'system' and the other, but also mentally and emotionally.*
- *It usually takes time for parents to find the best method of changeover for their children.*
- *Different strategies for changeover will be needed for low-, moderate- and high-conflict situations.*

Low-conflict situations

If your ex-partner is coming to your home to collect your children for their visit, you might like to invite them in for coffee. You might allow half an hour for the children to adjust to having the other parent present. The time can be spent asking the children about activities they have enjoyed with you or things they would like to do during their visit to their other parent. Importantly, this gives children time to prepare to say goodbye to one parent and adjust to the differences involved in staying with the other parent.

Some children will become distressed with both parents in one home. They sometimes respond better when the changeover occurs in a neutral place, such as a cafe or playground. Both parents can sit and have coffee for half an hour or so, giving the children time to adjust to being around the other parent before they go home with them.

Parents might also arrange for the changeover to take place at school. For many children, this is not a good idea, as changeover can be very upsetting and most children will not want their friends to witness their distress. In some families, however, it works well and is a method that some children really like.

Families can arrange for one parent to collect the children from school at the end of the school day (for example, on Friday afternoon) and return them to school on the morning of the agreed day (for example, on Monday morning). This allows the children to settle into familiar routines and friendships at school before having to readjust to living with their other parent.

Parents can also arrange to deliver any items to the other parent's home after they have dropped the children at school. This has worked well for families where the children have become severely distressed at changeover (finding it hard to let go of the parent they were staying with and reacquaint themselves with the parent they are due to stay with). For them, seeing both parents at the same time is too difficult and something for which they are not ready.

In a nutshell... Tips for changeover in low-conflict situations

- *When changeover occurs in the home, children need time to say goodbye to one parent and adjust to the presence of the other.*
- *A neutral location may be better if children become distressed with both parents in one home.*
- *In families where children find it hard to see both parents at the same time, changeover might take place at school.*

Moderate-conflict situations

Sometimes a mutual friend or supportive relative who is neutral to both sides might act as a 'go-between', transporting children from one parent's home to the other. If parents are considering this option, they need to ensure that the adult is someone the child feels comfortable with and whom the child and both parents trust. If the child feels uncomfortable with the adult, or the adult is unfamiliar to them, this can provoke anxiety and distress in the child, making changeover times traumatic. It is also important to check the adult's level of commitment. Children need predictability, so if the adult is unwilling to commit to the arrangement for very long, parents need to find another option.

If parents are in the habit of niggling, arguing or bickering at changeover times, again it might be helpful to consider a neutral location. However, this will work only if parents are unlikely to 'cause a scene'. Most adults will 'behave themselves' in public - and their children therefore won't have to fear that they will argue in the shopping centre, for instance, and humiliate or distress the children. Humiliating or distressing children (especially in a public place) will only serve to increase their dread of changeover times and lead them to feel more anxious about them.

A cafe, a park or a friend's home are all examples of neutral places that might be used.

In a nutshell... Tips for changeover in moderate-conflict situations

- *A trustworthy mutual friend or supportive relative, with whom the children feel comfortable, might act as a 'go-between'.*
- *If parents are in the habit of arguing at changeover times, a neutral location for changeover might be considered.*

High-conflict situations

In high-conflict situations where parents might be violent towards one another, more drastic strategies may need to be employed. If this applies to you, rather than engaging in discussion with your ex-partner, you might choose instead to send them a letter, or an email, outlining any information they need to know about the children, for their visit. The letter might contain details about the children's needs; any appointments that have been scheduled for the children during the visit (a doctor's appointment, for instance); any relevant information about their schooling; information about their visit to you; and things you observed in the children that you think your ex-partner might need to know (the onset of bedwetting, for example).

This option works well if parents find it impossible to communicate without this escalating into fights, arguments or violence. It minimises the interaction between them, and therefore the opportunities to argue.

In some countries, changeover at times of access in high-conflict situations might be overseen by organisations, such as social work/social welfare agencies. These may have developed programmes and employ staff specifically to assist parents in changeover. They may also have strategies in place to request police standby if required, and other security procedures. If available, this might be a favourable option for parents engaged in high conflict, or who have concerns about interacting with their ex-partner. It is also possible that local governing bodies and police stations may have services available to facilitate the safe 'handover' of children at access times. However, such services will vary from country to country, and possibly even from region to region.

In a nutshell... Tips for changeover in high-conflict situations

- *In situations of high conflict, parents might choose to communicate by letter or email.*
- *In some countries, social work/social welfare agencies may have programmes and staff to assist parents at changeover.*

Summary

Parents need to review and be willing to adapt their method of changeover, as children adjust to the separation, and as the needs of both children and parents change over time. Parents also need to accept when one method is not working and be willing to negotiate a different option.

Adopting a different method of changeover is not a sign of failure. As has been mentioned, parents often need to experiment with various methods before they find the one that works best for their family. Even then, the outcome may not be perfect, but 'good enough'. Separation is a very emotional process and grief can make changeover very difficult for families, despite parents' best efforts to find a suitable arrangement.

Depending on the age of the children, parents might want to involve them in discussions about methods of changeover. Children will often know what will work best for them and what they would prefer. They may suggest an option themselves that will suit the whole family and be easy for other family members to adjust to. If you would like to include your children in such discussions, allow them to decide whether or not they want to be involved. You might invite them either to participate or to decide between a number of options. It is important to bear in mind, though, that it is not a child's job to 'come up with a solution' and some may feel pressured or overwhelmed by being asked. Ultimately, it is the parents' responsibility to make the decision, and care needs to be taken about involving children.

Sometimes children will not want to attend access visits. There could be many reasons for this. It is important that you stay focused on building a long-term relationship with your children, so don't allow such thoughts as 'My child doesn't want to see me' to dishearten you or tempt you to give up. For both your sakes, you need to stay involved and keep up contact. Accept shorter visits if necessary, and be aware that children might feel torn between both parents, or be frightened that arguments might occur at changeover.

Allow your children to bring special items or toys to access visits with you, and when they leave, give them something of yours to 'hold on to' until you see them again. Plan access visits and remind the children of when you will see each other again. Stay in touch by telephone, email or letter. Some parents like to send a CD or a video/DVD of them reading a goodnight story to their children. You might also play games via the internet. Plan what you want to say and keep asking questions - for example, 'How was school?'; 'What's your homework tonight?' It is important to remember, too, that teenagers are often uncommunicative. Getting a one- or two-word reply from them is very typical (even in intact families), so don't take it personally. Continue to make contact and keep the channels of communication open.

Visits with your child: a summary of points to consider

- Give your children plenty of notice of upcoming visits, especially if they will be staying overnight. Don't tell them at the last moment: they need time to prepare for a visit, both practically and emotionally.
- If they are with you, but due to visit their other parent, stop any activities they are involved in ahead of time, rather than trying to pull them away from a computer game, for example, at the last moment. Allow them time to disengage from what they are doing and to prepare for their stay with their other parent.
- If their upcoming visit is with you, talk to them about it. Ask them what they would like to do during their time with you. Give them information on what they can and can't expect from you.
- Address any concerns your children might have about the visit. Be willing to be flexible if the

visit coincides with an event a child has been looking forward to, such as a friend's sleepover or birthday party.

- When your children come to visit you, allow them to bring with them some things that remind them of their other parent, or belong to their other parent.
- Never force a child to visit if they don't want to. Be patient.
- Some children will want to start with short visits and work their way up to overnight stays or consecutive day stays. Be flexible and allow them to set the pace they feel comfortable with. Keep this in mind when negotiating access.
- Allow your children to cut a visit short if they want to. Don't put your desire to spend time with them ahead of their needs or capacities. Sometimes children will seem fine, but then suddenly become distressed and want to return to their other parent. Don't take it personally. They are grieving and it will take time for their emotions to settle. Respect your children's needs.
- Trust is important. Don't cancel visits or make promises you can't keep. Your children are going through separation, just as you are, and they

need stability from you now more than ever.

- Allow your children to talk about their other parent. You might want to leave your ex-partner in the past, but she or he remains 'Mum' or 'Dad' to your children. Show respect for your children's relationship with their other parent.
- Allow your children to telephone or email their other parent while they are staying with you.
- Ensure that boundaries, routines and household rules are kept in place. Indulging children by dispensing with limits won't compensate for the grief feelings they are experiencing.

- Attempt to keep as many routines and rules the same between houses. Children find it easier to follow one set of rules, rather than having to adjust to different methods in different homes. If this is not possible, consider what you might be able to keep consistent for them.
- Provide a space for your children, so that they feel comfortable in your home. This is particularly important for older children. They require a room they can make their own, with a door they can close for privacy and personal space. Allow them to fill the room with their belongings.
- At the risk of having two of everything, provide your children with the practical things they need, to minimise the amount they need to bring with them each time they come to stay.

Ways in which parents can care for themselves through changeover

Some common triggers of distress and strategies for coping

Parents will often feel distressed when they witness their children being upset at changeover. While most parents will appropriately conceal their pain, in order to comfort their children, they too need support and comfort. If you are in this situation, allow yourself some private time to cry and feel sad, talk to a friend, or go for a walk and release pent-up emotions.

Talk to your children before changeover. Explain to them that changeover is often upsetting for children and adults alike, and that you and your ex-partner are doing your best to make it as smooth as you can. You might also want to tell them that sometimes you find it upsetting too. Doing so will help to normalise their feelings and let them know that it is all right for them, you and their other parent to feel upset for a while.

Many parents grieve and feel lonely when their children are visiting the other parent. Some find the house so quiet and unsettling when their children are not at home that they don't quite know what to do with themselves. It takes time for parents to adjust to the changes occurring in their family and to accept that their children won't be living with them all the time. That realisation in itself is enough to trigger a grief response of its own - it is a real loss for parents. Most parents don't want to miss one moment of their children's lives.

This is especially hard for parents who have few interests and hobbies beyond their children and family. For many parents, realising that most of their energy has been tied up in their family can be very difficult to deal with, and can leave some parents feeling empty: they live for their children and when the children are not at home they have nothing in their lives. For parents in this situation, who would like some help with processing the changes that separation has brought about for them, receiving support from qualified counsellors might be beneficial.

When their children are away, parents can take the opportunity to gradually grow used to 'their time' and begin to take up their own interests and hobbies again, or explore new ones. They might also look for things they can do for themselves that will be nurturing and enjoyable. These might range from warm baths and relaxing music, for example, to support groups and networks, visits to friends, exercise and meditation. Having time out from grief and being able to feel good within yourself are things that may take time to create and experience.

Having contact with an ex-partner can in itself be distressing and bring about renewed feelings of grief - especially if the separation is recent and was initiated by the other partner.

Again, most parents will attempt to conceal their pain for the sake of their children, and then quietly fall to pieces when they are alone. When this happens, they need to take action and call on all the support they have available to them.

This support may be in the form of friends, relatives or a counsellor. If this is happening to you, ensure that you have as many people as possible to call on, because relying constantly on just one or two friends for support can be wearing for them. Having a number of people on 'standby' means that you can move between them frequently. In this way, many people give you a little support and don't feel tired or worn out by your grief. Usually, it has been easier for women than for men to create support systems for themselves and contact a counsellor, but increasingly men are doing this more often - in some cases, more frequently than their ex-partners. By setting up a system of support, both partners will be well on the path to processing their grief in healthy ways.

Both you and your ex-partner will have unique and special gifts to offer. Your styles of parenting are likely to be different, but each of you will have a unique bond and relationship with your children. Avoid comparing yourself with your ex-partner. Thoughts such as 'My ex-partner is doing a better job of parenting than I am', or 'Maybe the children will be better off without me', are not helpful. Parenting takes practice and time. If much of it was previously done by your ex-partner, you may still be learning.

Have faith in your potential. Do things to regain trust in

yourself and confidence in your parenting. Take a parenting course, read a parenting book, make a list of parenting qualities that are special and unique to you. You are important to your children, who want and need you. Indeed, they need to have a positive relationship with both of their parents.

In a nutshell... Caring for yourself during changeover times

- *Parents will often feel distressed when their children are upset at changeover.*
- *Many parents grieve and feel lonely when their children are visiting the other parent, but this is also a time when they can begin to explore their own interests and hobbies.*
- *It is important that parents have as much support as possible to call on when grief resurfaces.*
- *Neither parent should compare themselves with the other: both will have unique gifts to offer their children.*

Role models

Children can feel isolated when they don't have sufficient contact with parents, or role models of both genders. Therefore, following family separation, it can be very helpful for children to have available to them a range of potential role models from which to choose, including members of the extended family, trusted family friends, older peers and mentors.

Mentors

Free mentoring programmes for children who are experiencing family separation might be run by large counselling organisations in your country. These might be run along the lines of a 'buddy' system and may last for varying lengths of time. Having a mentor who spends regular time with them provides children with an excellent opportunity to talk about their thoughts and feelings. It allows a relationship of friendship and respect to develop. Over time, children will often come to feel that their mentor understands them and 'is there for them'. They feel supported and cared about.

A mentor might be especially beneficial to older children and teenagers, who will often prefer to relate to a peer than to their parents. Having someone they can look up to, and who may also provide a gender role model, can help to reduce feelings of isolation and rejection, two common experiences of older or teenaged children going through family separation.

Family role models

Members of the extended family can act as role models for children. They can listen, participate in activities, share in some parenting and act as a support. Children feel disappointed and let down when one or both parents are not accessible to them. As a way of sharing quality time and building closeness, they might have a mental 'list' of things they would like to do with each parent - for example, 'fishing with Dad' or 'watching a film with Mum'. However, because children often sacrifice aspects of their own needs in an attempt to protect and care for their grieving parents during separation, they might feel that there is no point in talking about the list, and therefore may not always reveal it. The truth is that parents are interested in their children's wishes and needs, and it is important that children are told this and can ask for what they need.

When parents are not available (one might be living away from the immediate area; another might be at work), members of the extended family might be called upon as 'substitutes'. If a relative is willing to 'fill in' for a parent, children feel valued. Their needs are met, if not by their parent, then by a loving family member. They learn that they don't have to discount their list and that someone has recognised that their needs are important. It invites them out of isolation: although they might not be able to 'go fishing' or 'watch a film' with their parent, it can still feel good to do so with a relative they like and look up to.

In a child's world, feeling connected to people other than their parents is important. As well as helping children to feel valued and significant, it tells them they are cared about. It helps to build their sense of self-worth and resilience, and teaches them to look for other ways of meeting their needs. In this way, it helps children adjust to their loss - to accept that separation has brought changes, and that these changes can be worked around to make them more manageable. Cousin Robert or Aunt Sarah might not be the same as 'Mum' or 'Dad', but it is nice to know they care enough and are willing to help out. In other words, it is helpful for children to know that there are other people who understand, and with whom they can build a relationship and have a sense of connection.

The more *quality* support networks that are available to children, the better. Allow your children to nominate the people they want as their support. Don't force them to go fishing with Grandpa if they don't want to: they might prefer to fish with Cousin Robert instead. Children will automatically gravitate towards the people with whom they feel the greatest connection. Allow them to decide. It is, after all, for them.

That family members can also provide important emotional support should not be underestimated. A child might feel more comfortable talking further about the separation with a relative than with a close family member. They might need to hear explanations from other sources. Just knowing that there are relatives to whom they can turn is important for children.

In a nutshell... Role models

- *Mentors provide an excellent opportunity for children to talk about their thoughts and feelings.*
- *Children like to feel cared about by parents and significant other people: they need to know that others understand them and to feel a sense of connection with them.*
- *Children often have a list of activities they want to share with each of their parents. When parents are not available, relatives might be called upon as 'substitutes'.*
- *Quality support networks are important to children, who should be allowed to nominate the people they want as part of them.*

Becoming an 'I' again: re-establishing your independence

In relationships, individuals learn to connect to others. The identity they have as an individual, which allows them to operate as an 'I', merges with the 'I' of another person, to form a 'we'. This integration allows a couple to develop their shared identity, and to form an identity for themselves within that relationship. Healthy relationships involve a balance between 'I' and 'we'. Each person still has an individual identity and sense of self, which they balance with their relationship. They know who they are 'inside' and they feel 'connected to' themselves. In other words, they can feel full and complete within themselves, and enjoy a healthy sense of who they are. When a relationship ends, people enter a period of grief. They grieve the end of the 'we' they were a part of and begin to separate from it. When they emerge from their grief, they disconnect from the 'we' and re-establish their sense of 'I'.

Sometimes, however, in the process of becoming a 'we' people can lose sight of their 'I'. They lose their sense of self and identify themselves only through their relationship. What happens to such people when their relationship ends?

Some jump straight into another relationship, to fill the void left by the previous one. The prospect of being alone, even for a short while, frightens them. They avoid grief, in part or completely, and the process of disconnecting from the 'we'. They simply find someone else with whom to become a 'we', thereby avoiding establishing themselves as an 'I'. Others might choose instead to cling to their ex-partner, desperately attempting to maintain closeness and regain the shared identity they had before. In both these instances, the people concerned don't allow themselves to discover who they are or how to operate as individuals. Yet others are left feeling simply lost and empty. After a period of grief, they still feel unsure of who they are and unaware of how they lost themselves during the relationship. If they don't rebuild their identity, they run the risk of 'floating' and, without a sense of self, they too will identify themselves through their next relationship.

In other instances, people may develop addictions to mask their lack of identity. These addictions are used to numb feelings, and might include addiction to drugs, food, alcohol, shopping, exercise, gambling, excessive partying, smoking and risk-taking behaviour. Someone might also become addicted to cosmetic surgery, for example, and focus on improving their physical appearance (their 'external'), rather than on rebuilding within and establishing their identity. These methods provide temporary comfort and can alleviate the fear and anxiety associated with loss of identity. The problem, however, is that the anxiety returns. Addictions are short-term 'solutions' and don't work in the longer term. They are also potentially harmful and can further erode people's self-esteem and well-being.

Disconnection from ourselves occurs when we turn to others to make us feel complete. We allow the other person to become our source of love, affection, approval, acceptance and protection. We detach from our ability to meet our own needs, by expecting our partner to meet them for us and to 'complete' us. When we want to feel loved, we turn to our partner to give us love. We forget how to love ourselves (by treating ourselves in loving and accepting ways). What we don't use, we lose. This includes our ability to function independently.

If you have lost your sense of self during the course of being a couple, there are things you can do to reconnect to yourself. The process of becoming an 'I' again begins with turning within, to your core. Every person is ultimately responsible for themselves and for meeting their own needs. Fill yourself up so that you don't function from a place of need. Everything you need or want, you can give to yourself. When you are full and complete in yourself, you can accept what others give you, but what they give is not vital to your well-being. You can cope and function just as well if they don't give to you. Therefore, what you receive from others becomes an added bonus to an already 'full' you. You can function with the other person, but you can also function without them. You love them, but you love yourself more. They don't provide a measure of your self-worth.

Reconnect to yourself, therefore, by thinking about who you are at your core. Ask yourself what you like, dislike, prefer, want or desire. What choices and decisions have you made? What are your opinions and preferences? What are your interests and hobbies? Where do your qualities, strengths and natural talents lie? What kind of person are you? What makes you 'you'? What kind of personality do you have? What do you enjoy? What makes you feel alive? What makes you feel most connected to yourself? What do you love about yourself?

Begin by giving yourself the things you have wanted others to give you. Have you wanted affection, respect and acceptance? If so, now is the time to practise giving those things to yourself. Have you wanted to be heard and have your opinions listened to? Then start asking yourself what you think, and what your preferences are. Becoming an individual and gaining your own unique sense of 'I' starts when you allow yourself to make time for 'you'. This time is for connecting to yourself. You can use it to try out new things and discover different parts of yourself. Setting aside time for yourself allows you to become a priority in your life, and when you value yourself, you set the benchmark for others to value you too.

Remember that little eyes watch you and mirror you. Your children observe how you behave, what you believe about yourself, and how you cope with and adjust to change. If you can learn to meet your own needs, then you operate from a feeling of fullness. When you are full within yourself, you can give to your children more easily. When you are 'running on empty,' all you can think about is how 'hungry' you are and how desperately you want others to 'fill you up'. By giving to yourself, your children can benefit from having a parent who feels present, full and self-accepting. Choose to develop your own positive self-regard. Balance your ability to care for yourself with your important role of being a caring and responsible parent to your children. Developing a healthy sense of self, while being an accountable parent, is one of the best gifts you can pass on to your children - and it will teach them to feel good about who they are too.

No person is 'an island': various channels of support exist to help you develop these skills. As this book has mentioned earlier, while you are grieving, you can access grief counselling or post-separation counselling to help you to process your grief. As your grief recedes and you feel ready to embark on becoming an 'I' again, you can receive counselling to help you develop your sense of self, so that you emerge as an individual. Most importantly, you can also call on your friends and relatives for support, or turn to self-help groups, courses or other resources. Each of these can help you on your path to healing and towards becoming an 'I' again. It is a matter of finding the method that works best for you.

Everyone will have their own definition of what their 'I' looks and feels like. Therefore, only you can know when you arrive there. Developing your independence is likely to be a gradual process and you may experience some 'ups' and 'downs' as you separate the 'we' from the 'I', alternately feeling more like one or the other. Eventually, you will establish an independence you feel comfortable with. The duration of the process will be different for everyone and will depend on the extent to which you lost your sense of self within your former relationship. If you identified yourself only through your relationship, the process may take longer than if you felt connected to yourself from the beginning.

If you think you have lost your sense of self in the relationship, don't punish yourself or feel bad about it. Instead, find comfort in the knowledge that you can change things now. Many people lose their sense of identity and this often happens very gradually. First, they put one part of themselves away, and then another, until they realise that they have hidden so much of themselves that they don't realise who they are any more. They might have begun to identify themselves through the roles they have in the relationship, such as 'husband', 'father', 'wife', 'mother' or 'partner'. If this has happened to you, then you connected to a role, at the expense of yourself, rather than remaining connected to yourself and viewing those roles as extensions of yourself. But that was in the past, and now you are able to rebuild your identity and connect to yourself again by choosing to do things differently, with the skills, tools and knowledge you are gaining to help you do so.

When you re-establish your independence, acknowledge this to yourself. You could choose to mark it with a celebration or a ceremony to signal your passage from 'we' to 'I'. It is a significant milestone and deserves to be noted!

In a nutshell... Becoming an 'I' again

- *In relationships, the identity people have as individuals, which allows them to operate as an 'I', merges with the 'I' of another person, to form a 'we'; healthy relationships involve a balance between the two.*
- *Sometimes, however, people lose sight of the 'I' and need to find ways to reconnect with it following separation.*
- *As people emerge from grief, they are ready to function as an individual once more, by giving to themselves and rebuilding their identity.*
- *When a person is complete in themselves, what others give them is not vital to their well-being or sense of self.*

The benefits of post-separation services for a changing family

Post-separation counselling, mediation and conciliation are just some of the services available to separating families. This section provides some general information about these.

Each service functions in a slightly different way, and has different parameters and methods guiding the way it operates. However, in the main, the primary aim of post-separation services is to help separating families communicate during a time that is often stressful and difficult for some, if not all, family members. A neutral professional can help families to identify the main issue(s) they want to address, support them in exploring options, and assist them in selecting the option(s) that best fit their situation.

These services work well when both parties can negotiate on a level playing field, with the aim of making decisions that are mutually satisfactory and in the best interests of their children. Naturally, parents want to make decisions that will best suit their children's needs; however, in times of great stress and emotional grief, discussions between parents can often 'go off at a tangent' and become clouded. Both parents are hurting, grieving and feeling confused. They want to make sound decisions, but they also don't want to lose too much of what they value (contact with their children; financial means, for example). Therefore, conflict can easily arise. A power struggle can set in, as 'win—lose' dynamics take hold.

When people think they are about to lose something they value, they hold their ground, which may result in an impasse. The situation becomes 'stuck'. Professionals who work in post-separation services are trained to support parents through this. They help them to remain focused on finding workable solutions that are in the best interests of their children and themselves.

As part of this process, the children themselves can be consulted by specialised child consultants. The information gained in children's sessions can be carefully discussed with parents. This helps them to consider their children's perspective – what they are experiencing, feeling and wanting – from a different angle and enables them to keep the children's developmental needs in focus and to make informed decisions (McIntosh, 2007). Professor Jennifer McIntosh pioneered and researched this "child inclusive" way of resolving disputes (2007). Her website, ChildrenBeyondDispute.com, describes the approach in detail, with many supporting resources. Below is a summary of the main ideas.

In general, children will be asked to draw some pictures, aimed at helping them express their perceptions, feelings, worries, wants, needs, and so on. (The next section talks about interpreting children's drawings and what can be learned from them.) Play therapy might also be used, as children use toys to demonstrate aspects of their changing family life. 'Feeling' cards and other resources might also be utilised. Children will be asked questions and provided with a safe, child-friendly environment in which to discuss their views with a caring professional. Confidentiality, limits to confidentiality, and the aims of the sessions will be explained to both the parents and the children. Additionally, children will be asked what they especially want their parents to know, or not to know, about what they have discussed.

Parents might wonder initially why they can't just ask their children themselves, and bypass the process. Although parents are encouraged to keep communication pathways with their children open, it is important to realise that children don't want to upset their parents. As we have seen, they worry that if they discuss the separation with 'Mum' or 'Dad', it could upset them further. Children don't like to see their parents hurting. For the purpose of post-separation counselling, allowing children to meet with a trained child consultant can produce some insightful information that parents might not have gained otherwise, had they attempted to question their children themselves. Children will often open up to a 'neutral' person far more easily than they would to their own parents. They are not worried about upsetting the child consultant and so feel freer to reveal what they really feel and want.

The child consultant is trained in how to ask questions without producing unwanted side-effects such as stress, distress, pressure or shame. Children are helped to feel included. They are given the opportunity to describe their experience of the separation and to ask questions about the changes to their family. Their involvement helps them to feel empowered and heard. They like knowing that what they say can help to shape some of the outcomes or changes that will take place in their family. They are not made to feel responsible and it is made clear to them that their parents will make all decisions about the future of their family. Children are also informed that while their parents might not be able to meet all of their needs, their wishes will be heard by them and taken into account during post-separation discussions. Children often come away feeling very positive about their sessions with a child consultant, and usually report feeling good about being included in the process.

In a nutshell... The benefits of post-separation services

- *Post-separation counselling, mediation and conciliation are just some of the services available to separating families.*
- *Families can be helped to identify the main issue(s) they want to address, to explore options and to make decisions.*
- *Children themselves can be consulted by specialised child consultants.*
- *The information gained in children's sessions can help parents to understand what their children are experiencing, feeling and wanting, and to make informed decisions.*
- *Children often come away feeling very positive about their sessions with a child consultant, and about being included in the process.*

Interpreting responses: what we learn from children's diagrams

Three main questions are commonly asked of children by child therapists during post-separation counselling. These refer to: (1) how children saw their family before the separation; (2) how they see their family now that their parents are separating; and (3) how they would like their family to look. The following pages contain examples of diagrams often drawn by children in response to these questions. It can be difficult for parents to see such pictures, but the purpose is not to shame or upset them. Rather, it is to help them see the situation through their children's eyes. Children don't have the coping strategies or the thinking skills that adults have, so their views and perceptions will be different. Child therapists can help explain the diagrams, focusing on what the children want and need from their parents, so that, as mentioned above, parents are better able to consider, from a different angle, what is happening in their family (McIntosh, 2007; ChildrenBeyondDispute.com).

When you look at the pictures, note not only what the children have drawn, but the message or underlying need they are trying to express. It is this *need* or *want* that parents are encouraged to focus on and address, because this is what children are trying primarily to communicate. They are trying to tell their parents how their parents can help them. Parents can be empowered by recognising that there are things they can do straight away to give this help. This is not about going backwards or attempting to undo the past: the family is changing and that is the reality. Rather, it is about looking forwards to the important role parents have in their children's life, and how they can help to address their immediate needs. By being responsive to children's needs, parents can help them through the changes they are experiencing. Understanding and supporting their children at this stage can have powerful effects later on: they are helping to build a stronger family, based on positive new family dynamics for the future.

Question 1: How did you see your family before the separation?

Draw a picture.

[Diagram 1 (a)]

[Diagram 1 (b)]

Question 2: How do you see your family now that your parents are separating?

Draw a picture.

[Diagram 2 (a)]

[Diagram 2 (b)]

Question 3: How would you like your family to look?

Draw a picture.

[Diagram 3 (a)]

[Diagram 3 (b)]

Notice the similarities between the pictures in each category. Many children draw very similar pictures in response to the questions.

Younger children (aged 5-8) tend to draw simplistic diagrams, usually comprising stick figures with one or two distinguishing features; for example, Dad wearing his favourite hat. They will use several colours. They generally take between 5 and 10 minutes to draw one picture. In post-separation counselling they ask fewer questions and need less information.

Older children (from 9 years upwards) tend to draw more detailed pictures. For example, when drawing a house, they tend to draw in the bricks, rather than just an outline of a house. They usually take between 10 and 15 minutes to draw one picture. They will use fewer colours than younger children, sometimes choosing just to draw with a lead pencil. They show attention to detail and, in post-separation discussions, have a greater number of questions and want more information. When drawing pictures of their family prior to separation, children in this age group often draw members of their family with full, robust bodies. They might use bright colours. In contrast, diagrams of family members post-separation are usually drawn in stick figure form - a shadow of their former selves, in dull or few colours.

Children are insightful and use symbolism to reflect their feelings. They highlight very effectively the impact that family separation has on them and on other family members. For example, they will often draw a sun, a rainbow, birds, flowers, trees and smiling faces to represent togetherness in their family. They will usually draw dark clouds, rain, lightning and thunderbolts, or a scary animal such as a shark, to represent separation. They might also draw pictures of being trapped in water, or alone down a hole, to demonstrate images of their family during separation and to emphasise their feelings of vulnerability.

It is important that children are asked about their pictures - about what particular things they have drawn mean to them. When they draw members of their family, they should be asked about these family members first, rather than direct questions about themselves. This is a softer method of engaging children. Words should never be put into a child's mouth, however. Questions should be prompting - encouraging children to open up about their pictures, and always allowing them to talk about what they have drawn. For example, they might be asked: 'Is that Dad over there?'; 'What's he doing/feeling?'; 'Now, where are you? You look as though you are some distance from Dad: tell me about that'; 'Where would you like to be?'; 'How can Dad help with that?'

Whereas understanding pictures is more subjective and open to interpretation, written responses to exercises will be straightforward to interpret, because they will respond directly to the questions being asked.

In a nutshell... What we learn from children's diagrams

- *Children and adults will view things differently. Interpreting children's diagrams will help adults to see the situation through the children's eyes.*
- *Younger children tend to draw simplistic diagrams, whereas older children will draw more detailed pictures.*
- *Children use symbolism to reflect their feelings and the impact that family separation has on them and on other family members.*
- *It is important that children are asked about the meaning of their drawings.*

Parenting together after separation: creating dynamics for a new family

Your family is still a family following separation, but the dynamics are different. It will take time to define and create dynamics that work effectively for your 'new' family, and it will probably involve some trial and error. It will also take time for everyone to adjust to the changes. Your children will look to you for answers. They will want you to tell them what your family will look like now. They will want clarity, and to know when they will see each parent and what the role of each parent will be. Will both households have the same rules? Will family routines be upheld, or new ones developed? Are your parenting styles going to stay the same or will each of you parent in different ways now?

Naturally, you will not have all the answers straight away. Begin by telling your children what you are certain about, and tell them the rest as you work it out. You and your ex-partner will always be 'Mum' and 'Dad' to your children, and that tie will always bind you. Because of this, there will be an aspect of 'being together' even after separation. The degree to which that occurs will depend on the family itself and on the nature of the relationship between family members.

Counselling support could be beneficial at this point in the process. It could help you and your ex-partner forge a new direction for your family. The purpose will not be to cover old ground: this will not be relationship counselling aimed at reconciliation. Instead, it will be post-separation counselling, aimed at creating healthy new family dynamics for the future. The nature of the dynamics of your new family will be shaped by many things, including the areas of overlap between your life and that of your ex-partner. Common areas might be:

- your children, relatives and friends
- your home environment, suburb or community
- your finances, assets and careers
- your beliefs and willingness to establish a new family framework together
- other areas of life.

These and many other issues will shape the dynamics of your family post-separation. For example, imagine that a parent and their ex-partner owned a business while they were together. They worked well as a business team. In the late afternoon their two school-aged children would walk to the business after school and wait until they had closed for the day. Then they would all go home. A grandparent was at home caring for the youngest child who was pre-school age. During the day this grandparent cooked dinner for the family and they would all sit and eat the meal together. After dinner one of the parents would drive the grandparent home.

It is possible that following separation, not much has changed in this family. The parents may have decided they are still excellent business partners and can separate their 'business relationship' from their 'personal relationship'. They continue to work together in their business and it therefore makes sense that their children will continue to walk to the business after school. This allows the children to maintain their routine of seeing both parents daily. The grandparent might still baby-sit the youngest child, but because the family home has been sold and each parent lives elsewhere, the grandparent now looks after the baby at her home. She still cooks the evening meal, but now that is eaten at her home too. After dinner, each parent returns to their own home and the children go home with the parent they are scheduled to visit.

In this scenario, the routines the family had pre-separation are used as a platform to shape the dynamics of the 'new' family, post-separation. If the parents had not been able to maintain a business relationship following separation, however, it is possible that the dynamics might have changed drastically and new routines might have emerged. The family business might have been sold, and the parents might have forged new career paths individually. The children might therefore have had to attend after-school care and would no longer have seen both parents daily. The parent they were scheduled to visit on a particular day would have collected them from school, and other dinner arrangements would have been made. The grandparent might still have continued to care for the baby during the day.

These scenarios illustrate that the nature of post-separation family dynamics can indeed be influenced by many factors. It is possible for parents to define a version of 'staying together' after separation, but that version will depend on a range of such factors. Either way, the role of parenting the children and creating a new family dynamic is important, and will vary from family to family. There is no prescriptive way it should appear. If you are in this situation, you will need to be flexible and allow your dynamics to shift and change as you and your children change. Be willing to access counselling support to help you clarify the dynamics and boundaries, and be willing to try a few methods and variations until you strike the method that works best for your family. By involving all members of your family, including your children, perhaps through a child consultant, you can make decisions that incorporate the viewpoints of everyone. What a wonderful and empowering way for your family to recreate itself!

In a nutshell... Parenting together after separation

- *It will take time to create the dynamics of the 'new' family and for everyone to adjust to the changes.*
- *The nature of the dynamics of the new family will be shaped by many things, including the areas of overlap between one parent's life and the other's.*
- *Post-separation counselling can help clarify the new family dynamics and boundaries*

Resilience and building a stronger family

In life there will always be challenges. For children, it is possible that family separation is just the first of many challenges to follow. There are things you can do to help both your children and your family as a whole to build resilience. It is helpful to recognise that resilience emerges from encountering life challenges and from learning to adapt to change. Hence, becoming resilient is a skill we can all learn. Your family has this ability to adapt and move forward from separation. And, when faced with a later life challenge, you or your children will be able to look back at the separation and think, 'Well, I got through that and I'm okay, so I know I can get through this now.'

Four key methods to help families increase their resilience following family separation are:

- Positive self-regard: feel confident in yourself and your ability to handle life situations. Take care of yourself, pursue things you enjoy, and feel good within yourself. Look for opportunities to build your children's confidence and self-regard:

by pointing out situations they have handled, or are handling, well, and by helping them feel good about who they are and the unique talents and qualities they have.

- Positive regard for others: do things to show members of your family that they are loved, encouraged, supported, safe and cared about, and belong. Share quality time and activities with your children and take an interest in things they enjoy. Allow children to engage in a positive network of friendships and social activities. The healthy relationships your changing family has, both individually and collectively, can help each of you feel valued and connected.
- Healthy approach to change: focus on what you *can* change about the situation you are in. Help children feel empowered by encouraging them to make some decisions about small things they can change and improve. This helps children learn that although they can't change the situation, they can influence some things in their life to better meet their needs.
- Having plans and goals for the future: set small achievable goals and praise yourself for the steps you take each day towards achieving them. Give your children opportunities to accomplish small tasks and offer praise and encouragement

for their efforts. Children need to be given the opportunity to succeed at tasks: this helps them feel confident in themselves and powerful in their lives.

All these factors help children build confidence and a sense of well-being that can be drawn upon in other situations. These vital things are some of the key ingredients to developing resilience and skills for coping. In practising these things, you and your children might become aware of strengths you didn't know you had, including some shifts in the ways in which you perceive situations. You might notice that as your family progresses through the separation, you build and develop better channels of communication, affection, boundaries, problem solving, flexibility, assertiveness, and empathy for others, for example. Separation often promotes opportunities for change. As dynamics shift in the family, new styles of relating and new qualities and strengths emerge. These are things your family might not otherwise have gained.

As you can see, your family can become very resilient and adapt to the changes occurring within it. Each family member is unique and will want to be heard and accepted for who they are. They will want to feel connected to the people around them in a loving and safe way. Validating their feelings and experiences, praising them and providing consistency, boundaries, structure and rules will help your family to build resilience and feel secure.

When people feel secure they feel able to take risks, consider choices, make decisions, try different tasks and take on responsibilities. All of these things help people feel good about who they are and allow them to feel powerful and potent in their lives. Everyone wants to feel that they can accomplish things that are manageable and realistic for them. Whether this is managing feelings, dealing with a situation, learning something new, or connecting in a new way, developing a sense of 'I can do this' is a large part of what resilience is all about.

You are on your way to becoming the family you will be in the future. Every day you take one step closer to it, and shape and define it more strongly. Reflect on what you want your family to aspire to. What will be special and unique about your family, and what are the skills, strengths and resources you hope your family can develop and draw on? What is the most important thing you want for yourself and for your family?

Recognise the strengths you have as individuals and as a family today. Affirm those strengths and allow them to underpin the family you see yourselves becoming. Notice the ways in which you and your family emerge and grow through separation. Notice the ways in which you build resilience, collectively and individually, and become a stronger family and stronger individuals. As you navigate your way through the course of separation, notice how you are working together to create the family you want to be.

The canvas is blank, but what you do and what you decide from here will form impressions upon it. Therefore, aspire to create with intent, so the impressions you paint on the canvas are deliberate ones. Only you and your family can decide what you want and how you want to be. So ask yourselves the all-important question: 'Where do we want to go from here?'

(This section has been adapted in part with permission from The Road to Resilience https://www.apa.org/helpcenter/road-resilience. Copyright © 2011 American Psychological Association).

In a nutshell... Resilience and building a stronger family

- *Families can become very resilient and adapt to the changes occurring within them.*
- *Validating feelings and experiences, giving praise and providing consistency, boundaries and opportunities all help to make people feel secure and to build resilience.*
- *When people feel secure they feel able to take risks, consider choices, make decisions and take on responsibilities.*
- *Only you and your family can decide what you want and how you want to be. Aspire to create changes with intent.*

References

American Psychological Association, 2011, *The Road to Resilience*, online, https://www.apa.org/helpcenter/road-resilience.

Illsley Clarke J & Dawson C, 1998, *Growing Up Again, Parenting Ourselves, Parenting Our Children*, 2nd edn, Hazelden, Center City, MN. (First published in 1989.)

McIntosh J, 2007, ChildrenBeyondDispute.com

Bibliography/recommended reading

American Psychological Association, 2011, *The Road to Resilience*, online, https://www.apa.org/helpcenter/road-resilience.

Bieber JD, 1998, *If Divorce is the Only Way*, Penguin Books, Ringwood, Victoria.

Brooks R & Goldstein S, 2004, *The Power of Resilience: Achieving Balance, Confidence, and Personal Strength in Your Life*, McGraw-Hill, New York.

Green M, 1998, *Fathers after Divorce: Building a New Life and Becoming a Successful Separated Parent*, Finch Publishing, Lane Cove, New South Wales.

Henley L, 1994, *So Now You're on Your Own*, Ray Books/Harper Collins Publishers, Sydney.

Illsley Clarke J & Dawson C, 1998, *Growing Up Again, Parenting Ourselves, Parenting Our Children*, 2nd edn, Hazelden, Center City, MN. (First published in 1989.)

McIntosh J, 2007, *'Child inclusion as a principle and as evidence-based practice: applications to family law services and related sectors'*, AFRC Issues No. 1, 2007, Australian Family

Relationships Clearinghouse, Australian Institute of Family Studies, online, http://www.aifs.gov.au/afrc/pubs/issues/ issuesl.html.

McIntosh J, 2007, ChildrenBeyondDispute.com

Neuman MG, 1998, *Helping Your Kids Cope with Divorce the Sandcastles Way*, Random House, New York.

Pritchard R, 1998, *When Parents Part: How Kids Adapt*, Penguin Books, Auckland.

Ricci I, 1997, *Mom's House, Dad's House*, 2nd edn, Simon & Schuster, New York.

Schaefer D & Lyons C, 2001, *How Do We Tell the Children?*, 3rd edn, Newmarket Press, New York.

Seddon E, 2003, *Creative Parenting after Separation*, Allen & Unwin, Crows Nest, New South Wales.

Weyburne D, 1999, *What to Tell the Kids about Divorce*, New Harbinger Publications, Oakland, CA.

Websites

http://www.divorceandchildren.com

https://www.separatedfamilies.info/

http://www.familylives.org.uk/advice/divorce-and-separation/

https://kidshelpline.com.au

http://www.childrenbeyonddispute.com

http://www.apahelpcenter.org

Disclaimer

These books were written largely from the author's own understanding, based on extensive training in this field. However, generic related information can be found in the books and online sites that are mentioned in the bibliography and recommended reading list, to which readers can refer.

NB Where content has been included or adapted from other sources, genuine attempts were made to identify those sources, but some results were unsuccessful. If notified, the publisher will be pleased to rectify any errors or omissions at the earliest opportunity.

The publisher bears no responsibility for the persistence or accuracy of URLs for external or third-party internet websites referred to in this book, and cannot guarantee that any content on such websites is, or will remain, accurate or appropriate.

About the Author

Marina Tsioumanis has worked clinically with hundreds of separating families, providing specialized post-separation counselling to parents and children. She's taught hundreds of courses about grief, family separation, child development, personality development, communication, parenting skills and relationship skills.

Marina Tsioumanis (CTA) is a Certified Transactional Analyst, with Educational Specialty. She lectured in the nationally accredited Certificate IV in Counselling Skills with Transactional Analysis qualification for nearly a decade. She also taught professional counselling and psychotherapy skills to groups of Psychologists, Counsellors and Social Workers.

This is Marina's first published work and has featured in newspaper, television and magazine interviews in a number of countries. The first edition of the three-book series was Awarded 'Highly Commended' at the prestigious British Medical Association (BMA) Book Awards, 2009.

Marina lives with her partner and young daughter in the foothills of Adelaide, South Australia. She enjoys painting, cooking, reading, gardening, home decorating, and being surrounded by nature.

She can be contacted through publisher@newynpublishing.com

Printed in Dunstable, United Kingdom

65202568R00097